THE POWER OF RELATIONSHIP MARKETING

THE POWER OF RELATIONSHIP MARKETING

How to Keep Customers for Life

TONY CRAM

FT
PITMAN
PUBLISHING

PITMAN PUBLISHING
128 Long Acre, London WC2E 9AN

A Division of Pearson Professional Limited

© Longman Group UK Limited, 1994

First published in Great Britain 1994

© Tony Cram, 1994

British Library Cataloguing in Publication Data
A CIP catalogue record for this book can be obtained from the British Library.

ISBN 0 273 60907 6

3 5 7 9 10 8 6 4

Typeset by Northern Phototypesetting Co. Ltd, Bolton
Printed and bound in Great Britain by
Biddles Ltd, Guildford and King's Lynn

Ashridge is a charity number 311096 registered as Ashridge (Bonar Law Memorial) Trust

CONTENTS

For Chris, Joseph, Ben,
Ruth and Peter

INTRODUCTION

Your business plan is almost certainly based on winning and keeping new customers. Your competitors are probably actively seeking to recruit your customers. You may be finding that building relationships with your customers is the most important and also the most challenging task you face. The techniques of Relationship Marketing are crucial in achieving your commercial objectives. My purpose in this book is to share and develop from the theories behind relationship marketing, practical ideas that you can implement to keep your customers coming back.

My interest in relationship marketing began many years ago, with a preference for longer term customer strategies. I learnt from positive experiences at Unipart, Grand Metropolitan Plc and TSB Bank through the 1970s and 1980s. At that stage I had no label or descriptor. In September 1992, at Ashridge Management College, I met Regis McKenna, author of *Relationship Marketing – Own the Market through Strategic Customer Partnerships* (1991). He inspired me with a label – Relationship Marketing – and a framework which tallied closely with my own thoughts and experiences. Influenced by his clarity of thinking and expressive turn of phrase, I have extended practical applications of the operational aspects of relationship marketing.

His presentation also influenced Ashridge in the marketing of its own range of executive development programmes. In reviewing its own marketing approach in the light of this thinking, Relationship Marketing principles are being successfully adopted in developing the College's marketing strategy by Virginia Merritt and her team.

Marketing challenges are a frequent topic of discussion with the managers who come to Ashridge on public programmes, or courses tailored to the specific needs of particular organisations.

We have seen that many of these challenges are addressed by the application of relationship marketing. Whilst it is by no means a panacea, there are many practical techniques which can be applied in response to some of the pressures on marketing directors and managers. The subject is a consistent theme running through the **Marketing Management and Business Development** programme at Ashridge, and additionally during the programme, time is spent directly focusing on the subject. A short overview of **Relationship Marketing** is also available in 1995. The intensity and value of these sessions convinced us that there was a need for a practically orientated book on how to benefit from the power of Relationship Marketing. Thinking long term has an intellectual rigour in its own right. How you gain sway for and carry out this long term approach is another matter. This book was written in response to that need.

The book is structured in a particular sequence. Three sections are evident:

(i)   Setting the Scene
(ii) Seven Steps of Relationship Marketing
(iii) The Future of Marketing

Setting the scene – Chapters 1 to 4
We begin with an overview of the original process of marketing, following its development and metamorphoses until we find that delivery of the original values is being revived through technology. Relationship Marketing is defined. We look at the value of long term relationships and the cost of short term relationships. The interplay of the seven steps is introduced.

Seven steps to Relationship Marketing – Chapters 5 to 12
The steps as shown in Figure I.1 are described. In addition to communications, there is a special chapter on word-of-mouth marketing

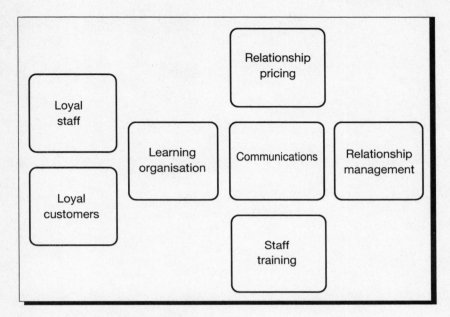

Fig I.1 Relationship marketing

The future – Chapter 13
Relationship Marketing is in essence, responsive or even anticipatory of change. This chapter looks at the way it may need to adapt and develop in future.

The book will have succeeded, if it helps you to enhance and develop your customer relationships further. You are a partner in this. You will need to recognise the areas where the ideas are directly applicable. You will have to manage their introduction and execution. In this way, you and I have a relationship, I hope that it is truly productive.

ACKNOWLEDGEMENTS

Any book has a team of people behind it. This book perhaps more than many. Hence I would like to thank the team who helped me develop and express these chapters. I would like to recognise the wealth of ideas that I have gained from discussions with my colleagues at Ashridge Management College, and the reliable test bed they have provided for my own thoughts. Directly or indirectly, many people have supported me in the thinking behind this book. My thanks are due also to the many programme participants at Ashridge for the stimulation their interest in the subject has provided me.

Thank you also to the *Harvard Business Review* for permission to reprint the excerpt from 'Spend A Day in the Life of Your Customers' by Francis J. Gouillart and Frederick Sturdivant (January/February 1994), copyright © 1994 by the President and Fellows of Harvard College; all rights reserved.

Thanks too, to Mark Allin, Trish Denoon and Joy Wotton, who have encouraged, challenged and supported me in this endeavour.

Chris, my wife, shared the experience with me, page by page and with this, improved the process and the book. Thank you.

Despite all the team work, advice and support, the views expressed and the mistakes are entirely my own.

1

MARKETING COMES
FULL CIRCLE

Two hundred years ago, the natural approach to the market was through Relationship Marketing. The early success of William Addis, who invented the toothbrush in 1780 and founded a business which continues today, was based on understanding and interacting with his customers. Jacob Schweppes, who founded the soft drink company in 1790 in Geneva, gained his early experience through relationships with local doctors who provided poorer patients with his sparkling mineral waters. In the nineteenth century, relationships with customers were essential to entrepreneurs like Henry Heinz selling his glass bottles of grated horseradish, Andrew Pears marketing his refined and delicate soap, and David H. McConnell direct selling perfumes under the Avon name. Relationship Marketing was the foundation of a successful business.

Marketing in its purest form existed in the town or village, with merchants and tradesmen marketing their wares. In a community, success as a baker, for example, depended on repeat business. This came from baking good bread and acting on a knowledge of the villagers' nature and preferences, leading to particular relationships with individual customers.

And then came mass markets

Individual markets were dramatically affected by the onset of mass media, leading to mass marketing and mass consumption. Manufacturing efficiencies combined with mass distribution channels and national media created homogenous markets. Products adapting well to the changed circumstances became dominant in their categories. For example, production volume and efficiency meant that no one could replicate the value of a Mars bar. Ubiquitous distribution and the impact of powerful advertising – 'A Mars a Day, Helps You Work, Rest and Play' – reinforced the brand's eminence. Mass markets increasingly became the norm during the twentieth century.

Now, this phase is ending. We are entering an era of change and development. Change is occurring in markets and marketing, and all the factors – political, economic, social – which impinge on marketing.

We shall look first at this new stage of change and development. Then we shall consider its progenitor, technology, and how that has created a global market. The consequences of a world market place are outlined to set the scene for the renaissance of Relationship Marketing. So we begin with our era of change.

The future is not what it used to be

Paul Valéry highlighted the new nature of change and development with his comment, 'the future is not what it used to be.' Predicting the future has always been a risky and uncertain endeavour. It begins with an understanding of the present and the forces shaping it. These trends are then extrapolated to create an image of the future. This future is seen as the next part of a process of continuous change. Invariably, there are some surprising threads to the pattern that unfolds. Now, however, the whole pattern is capable of change. In an era of discontinuous change, the future is not as predictable as it used to be.

Political and economic surprises

A landmark in the demise of predictability occurred in November 1989 with the fall of the Berlin Wall. The division of Europe had been a stable assumption for forty years. Suddenly, new markets opened, drastically lower labour costs became available to European managers, new countries emerged and war broke out in a European holiday destination. Who foresaw a war in Europe and an Arab–Israeli Peace Accord?

In the political environment forecasting is as difficult. Most opinion polls suggested a Labour victory in the UK election in April 1992 won by John Major. At the end of the Gulf War, George Bush was the most popular president in US history. Yet a year later, he lost the White House to a then little-known politician from Arkansas. In October 1993 the ruling party in Canada under Kim Campbell lost all but 2 of their 152 seats. Italian politics continue to twist in new and surprising ways.

Assumptions for the world economy soar or collapse according to different commentators. We have seen the pound, which in August 1992 would never leave the European Exchange Rate Mechanism, make its exit in September. The General Agreement on Trade and Tariffs, whose labyrinthine negotiations were supposedly doomed to fail, was signed by virtually all nations in December 1993. We now have an active North American Free Trade Area.

Unexpectedly the Rio Summit in June 1992 led to environmentalism being endorsed in person by more heads of state than any other initiative. Green Parties won tranches of votes. And now where are Green Politics?

Socially we have seen in many developed countries the steady decline in the importance of the family as a social unit. In North America and northern Europe, the nuclear family of father, mother and children is no longer a representative image. Yet the United Nations designated 1994 the 'Year of the Family' and the theme was taken up with more interest and enthusiasm than many other annual themes. British media adopted 'Family Values' as a real cause.

Media change is more rapid than many expected. New York is heading towards 500 television channels, explaining the popularity of Channel 47 which solely features programme listings of other channels. *The European* was flamboyantly launched as a new newspaper and struggled for acceptance. Meanwhile the *Financial Times* began publishing on the continent and became Europe's business paper. Ask someone you know, how many homes receive MTV in how many countries. Few will estimate the correct figures of 235 million homes across 87 countries. In Europe alone, MTV has 40 million regular viewers in the 16-to-34 year-old band.

A new direction for prices

For fifty years prices of most goods (other than commodities and high tech items entering volume production) have been downwardly inflexible. In August 1993 in London, a leading, highly differentiated premium quality brand – *The Times* newspaper – reduced its cover price initially from 45p to 30p. The same has occurred for certain Italian and Japanese distinctive high-status motor marques. In industrial markets, price escalation clauses in new and long-term contracts are being replaced by prices which reduce over time in line with progress down the experience curve.

Technology reframes transport, travel and communications

For many of these changes and developments, technology is directly or indirectly, the driving force and explanation. Technology has impacted dramatically on costs and capacity of transportation, travel and communications. Together these three factors have created a global market.

Let us look first at the impact of technology on transport and how this has opened up a global potential. Transportation in the 1990s would be unrecognisable to a stevedore of the 1950s. New designs of massive capacity container ships, with rail and road links to hinterlands, and cost-effective jumbo jet airfreight have expanded choice of goods exponentially. Seasonality of fruit, flowers and vegetables has been replaced by year round availability in supermarkets. New fruits, like starfruit, rambutans and kumquats appear alongside the traditional favourites. Country of origin labelling demonstrates globalisation in a single aisle of a hypermarket.

As an exercise, look in your kitchen and count the different countries which have contributed to its structure and contents. Perhaps a door from Finland, tiles from Spain, wall paint from the UK or USA, sink and taps from Germany, linen from Eire, Swedish or Polish glassware, refrigerator from Italy, microwave from Singapore or Korea, miniature television from Japan or Indonesia, beer from Mexico or the Czech Republic, wine from South Africa, Bulgaria or California, apples from France, bananas from the Caribbean, Argentinian beef, Brazilian coffee, New Zealand butter. Six continents and more than twenty countries can be listed without difficulty. A global market in your own home.

Travel too has helped to create the global market. By placing international travel within the price bracket of millions, through low cost air travel in wide-bodied 500-seat jet airplanes, national tastes are becoming international. Experiences of products and services in another country become expectations back at home. Travellers also pass their ideas, needs and wishes to the host country. Australia's impact on Bali and Indonesia has been significant. Swedes holidaying in the Gambia have changed lifestyles in West Africa. You may not have visited Malaysia, Hungary or Panama yourself, but someone you know has done so.

Lastly, communications has played a major part in this trend to globalisation. Personal and business communications have been revolutionised by technology. From the telephone handset on your desk, you can call half a billion people in 186 countries around the globe, in every time zone. With a mobile phone, you can always be accessible. Globally there are 25 million facsimile machines, sending and receiving documents, locally, nationally and internationally. Messages can be left for you on an answerphone, a facsimile machine, or through electronic mail. France-Telecom's minitel system of domestic computer phone directories means that when a new number is issued or changed in France, every subscriber has reference to that change. If you are out of contact, it is by choice.

Information is retrievable, rapidly from libraries and databases across the world. Blackwell's, the Oxford bookseller, is now marketing under the name 'Uncover', access to 5 million articles culled from 14,000 magazines, to anyone with an Internet connection and a credit card. They are ordered by electronic mail and delivered by fax, maybe within one hour.

The fax machine can act as a near instant source of further information by suppliers and advertisers. The fax-back system allows an enquirer with a touchtone phone and a fax machine to dial into a supplier and request product or service details, without human intervention. The potential customer simply inputs a product code and a fax containing the information is automatically sent back. The journal, *Business Marketing Digest*, cites an international firm of architects and designers – DEGW – who send a monthly single-page fax newsletter to 2,800 clients and contacts worldwide.

The consequence of this massive development in telecommunications is to break down barriers and resistances. Everyone can be reached by communications. Information flowing freely means more rapid acceptance of new and improved products, services, ideas, and methods. Rapid, low cost and efficient communications globally are creating an international transparency and an international market.

So, technology has, through its impact on transport, travel and communications, created a world marketplace.

Before we look at the impact of technology on the mass markets of the 1960s and 1970s, we need to understand the consequences of this world marketplace. Global markets have global competitors. Global competitors have destroyed natural scarcity in almost every market outside gems and bullion. Capital, raw materials, labour and production capacity are more plentiful than ever before. There is no scarcity of capital for an investment which has the potential to pay back. Capital can flow freely within the European Union. It can move with minimal hindrance in most developed countries in the world. Japanese, British, Swiss and American banks are world players. Better production utilisation, design efficiency, miniaturisation and artificial substitutes even militate against raw material scarcities.

There is no scarcity of labour. Huge potential labour forces exist for products and services across the globe. Services like name and address file data input for direct marketing mailing lists can be carried out in India. Typesetting can be executed in Singapore. Garments designed on a computer screen in Los Angeles, appear on another screen in the Philippines where samples can be cut out, sewn together and air-freighted back to the USA within 48 hours. In most markets there is virtually no shortage of production capacity. For chemicals, cameras, cookers, clothing and cars, factories can more than meet current and expected demand. Europe has an overcapacity in passsenger vehicle production of 7 million units.

The only scarce commodity is buyers. Uneven income distribution means that affordability is the constraint for many would-be purchasers.

Overcapacity places on firms a competitive pressure to outperform rivals in order to survive. Competing dimensions are many and vary by product and industry. They can be categorised in terms of the following model:

Tangible benefits	**Intangible benefits**	**Price**
Examples	*Examples*	*Examples*
Speed, quantity,	Reputation, image,	Cost,
durability, weight,	reassurance,	discount,
variety, novelty,	style, acceptability,	credit
flexibility	environmentalism	

Focus on price based benefits can be short lived as a strategy. Being the lowest priced reel-to-reel tape recorder supplier is of little competitive value when the market has swung over to audio-cassettes. Beef burgers on credit terms are no match for a McDonalds if the waiting time is substantially longer. Whilst price is always a critical variable, it is the deciding factor when all else is equal. The tangible and intangible benefits ensure that all else is not equal.

Speed, flexibility and novelty

Tangible benefits like speed to customer, flexibility and novelty are often the most vital dimensions in industrial markets. Business buyers are seeking advantages for their own concerns. The message is 'help me to make my organisation succeed'.

Korean suppliers to Lucky-Goldstar are an extension of the production system through just-in-time delivery. Kirin guarantee to deliver their packaged beers to liquor stores within three days of brewing. DHL have based their business proposition on speed with reliability.

Flexibility is a competitive dimension which requires suppliers to update, vary, extend and miniaturise responsively and effectively. The symbiotic relationship between the successful UK retailer Marks & Spencer and their major clothing supplier Courtaulds is based significantly on this flexible responsiveness built into the arrangement.

The attraction of novelty is compelling in many circumstances. Life has moved on since 1900, when the then Director of the US Patent Office wrote recommending that the office be closed on the grounds that there was nothing left worth inventing! Now it is possible for a company in a hi-tech industry, like 3COM Corporation, to earn more than 50 per cent of its revenue from products launched in the previous two years. All companies must strive to ensure that their designs, processes and products are not rendered obsolete by industry developments. The progressive Europe-wide launch of the Magnum ice cream bar raised the stakes for all the domestic competitors in the individual countries. Will 'Dry Beers' or 'Ice Beers' radically alter the beer market? Novelty carries its own intrinsic attraction for a minority. For a majority, the performance benefits it can bring make the attraction more pragmatic.

The consequence of the drive for competitive excellence in speed and flexibility is a pressure on processes, costs or both.

The pressure for novelty

The pressure for novelty carries a double pressure. Firstly it increases development costs as a proportion of total expenditure. The American Pharmaceutical Association have estimated the cost of developing a single new drug and bringing it to market is in the order of $231 million.

Secondly, the urge for continuing novelty also implies a shorter payback period. Only now is the Japanese motor industry retreating from its ever shorter vehicle turn time. At one stage existing models were being superseded within 27 months of launch. New and more costly development initiatives are aimed at fickle markets where flexibility, speed and enhanced performance attributes are required. It is a high stake endeavour.

Brand reputation as a defence

Intangible benefits of reputation, reassurance and image are vital aspects of the need for competitive excellence and differentiation. Arguably they are more vital than ever, in that for many manufactured products, replicability in performance terms from rivals is a real threat. How can one brand of industrial carpet create a real product difference from another? What essentially distinguishes one camcorder from another? It goes beyond products and affects many services. If one bank launches an interest-bearing account with particular characteristics, or an insurance company develops critical illness cover, a competitor can have a rival version in the market within 24 hours. For this reason, soft benefits, associated with perceptions and brand image are as critical for successful differentiation as the hard product /service attributes.

Interestingly, these soft benefits frequently carry personal characteristics, as if the brand were actually a human being. For example, Pepsi Cola as a person would be seen as young, lively, spontaneous and active. Benetton would probably be as young, but bolder to the point of abruptness. Sony would be neat, efficient, precise and dependable. Thus it appears that whilst technology may create a mechanical process, it can inspire a re-emphasis on human values.

From mass market to mass customisation

Technology has brought into being a global marketplace. At the same time it has altered the characteristics of that marketplace. Specifically, it has brought about the end of the mass market in many categories. The era of mass marketing is ending, and a period of mass customisation is burgeoning.

In simple terms, a single flavour of Coca-Cola met the needs of the mass market from 1886 until 1982. There was a single significant change with the appearance of the shaped bottle in 1915. In the period since 1982, Diet Coke, Caffeine-free Coke, Cherry Coke and other permutations have been launched. There is a clear version called Tab, and a multiplicity of pack variants from cans to bottles to PET, in sizes from 200 ml to 3 litres. With the body shell, engine, transmission, trim choices, paint colours plus factory options, it would be possible for Land Rover to produce Discoveries for a year without repeating the same specification.

Three forces appear to be leading this sea change in market focus.

Firstly, companies are using choice as a dimension of competition. The full line-up proposition can be used to defeat a competitor without the power to compete in all sectors. Retailers are using this as a technique to grow at the expense of rivals and retailers in contiguous sectors. Thus the average Carrefour now carries 40,000 lines. The standard Safeway store in USA has over 120 different breakfast cereals. It is a choice explosion.

Secondly, the forms of mass communication which were the familiar stamping ground of the marketer of the 1970s are fragmenting. A single commercial television channel in many countries, has developed into two or three terrestrial channels. Cable has followed and satellite channels are now multiplying. Star TV has extended satellite options in South-east Asia and India. In the UK there is now a choice of around 16 TV channels and 100 commercial radio stations. The number of magazines available on European news-stands is now beyond counting, with particular growth in Italy, Netherlands and Belgium.

Thirdly, this media fragmentation has presented advertisers with a challenge. Reaching smaller audiences with mass media becomes increasingly expensive in terms of cost per thousand viewers. Money is saved by creating shorter advertisements. In USA, more than half the TV commercials aired have a duration of 15 seconds. In the UK, the *Guinness Book of Records* achieved its own first, with a 3-second television advert in December 1992.

This situation – shorter length adverts, more competing advertisers and more products to promote – is tending to lead to an advertising stridency which is counterproductive. Greater noise, drama and technical wizardry are conditioning viewers to notice the process more than the product. Particularly in consumer markets, cynicism has spread from advertising to sales promotion. Coupon malredemption, for example, is rife. Faith and trust in the retailing system is under threat from the dashed expectations of Total Quality and the broken promises of customer service commitments. In blunt terms, the mass consumer has been educated to be sophisticated about products and services, and cynical towards promises.

SUMMARY

- In essence, we have seen the progress of business towards mass marketing led by technology. We have seen technology create the world market. However, before the world could be treated as a mass market, technology, with its unpredictable consequences, has fragmented that market into myriads of categories, groups, segments, sub-segments and individuals. Those individuals have expectations and a dulled sensitivity to communication appeals of the mass marketing age.

- Where do we go from here?

2

RELATIONSHIP MARKETING

The same technological forces which have created a world market, with new media and a multiplicity of new products, are providing the solution. Technology has given us back the tools for individual marketing that existed in the main street or town square of bygone years.

Know your customer . . . individually

The plummeting real costs of computing and the exponential increases in software flexibility are making possible cost-effective databases. Through their database, Marriot Hotels can know the likes and dislikes of 5 million people – their favourite rooms, whether they expect an iron and ironing board, the newspaper they enjoy – and meet these expectations. Among major American hotel chains, Marriot has the highest occupancy rate.

Relational databases like Birmingham-based, TSB Bank's 'Customer Information Database' are the foundation of a new form of marketing. TSB Bank know what has been communicated to individual customers and how they have responded. What the customer receives is consistent and appropriate behaviour from a knowledgeable partner. The great destroyers of relationships – inconsistency, forgetfulness and inappropriate behaviour – are eliminated.

As the tradesman of 200 years ago knew his customers by

name, where they lived, their likes and dislikes, tastes and preferences, and so on, nowadays it is possible for a company to have the same level of data on customers. In the 1990s this is on an enormous scale. The recall and recognition is not a mental process, but a computer driven exercise. Billions of elements of data are related to millions of customers.

Create your own car specification

Technology gives more than this. Design, scheduling and production technology can create the opportunity for product customising. You can design your own Ford Mondeo with a personal permutation of body shell, engine size, colour, trim and option selection. According to Regis McKenna, the National Industrial Bicycle Company of Kukuba, Japan, can deliver a made-to-order bicycle within two weeks from a potential spectrum of 11,321,000 variants.

When the trader prepared his batches manually, he could deliberately prepare one tray with a particular customer in mind. Now there is almost ultimate flexibility within the parameters set down by computer aided design and control.

Individual follow up

After an advertisement is broadcast, instant product information is possible through faxback. There are more than a million fax machines in the UK. The technology exists to call up the fax number given at the end of an advert and receive back, automatically, a fax of further information, prices and a list of stockists. It is possible for retailers to offer regular customers account cards and then, using in-store monitors sensitive to the magnetic stripe, track and time their progress through the store. Customers can be sent offers and product information related to the merchandise in the departments where they spent the most time. In other words, the knowledge of the customers' interests can be used to select what is and is not communicated to make it appropriate.

This is another aspect of the form of marketing of old brought into today's world. In his market, the stall holder could present his wares differently to each customer. He could stress the quality of ingredients to one and the care and attention in the making to another. Normally he would have a range of messages for different groups. He could even tailor his message to a single person if need be. That flexibility now exists in the 1990s, where it is possible to create a segment of one person.

Recognising the individual

The trader would recognise his customers instantly. The same possibility now exists mechanically. When a customer faces a bank teller, the account number will call up the customer details on screen, to enable the teller to make reference to previous transactions, to enquire after the car which had been purchased recently with a bank loan. The teller can ask the customer if they have read mailings sent in the past week and offer to arrange further information if desired.

A major part of business to business marketing relies on telephone contact. The recognition facility exists now for telephone calls. With computer-integrated voice response, calls are answered by a computer which greets callers with a pre-recorded message. This will ask them for their account number to be input by touch tones. The voice response can also provide a guide to the length of the brief interval before connection to a person. The call will be automatically routed to the account manager for that customer. When he or she receives the call, they will automatically have full customer details on the screen of their PC.

Digital exchange lines can accommodate more than one number per line. Direct Dial Inward (DDI) telephone systems can permit callers to go directly to the work station of the person they seek without going via a switchboard. Through digital communications, the local exchange communicates which particular number is being called. By allocating an individual DDI number to each customer, it is possible to have calls automatically routed to the appropriate contact point and have their screen showing account and customer details.

Satisfying the individual

Both customer and vendor knew what was in stock on the market stall by means of a simple visual check. Mass marketing in an undifferentiated way always carried with it the danger that items out of stock might be offered to customers. This is a service failure. It is frustrating for the customer and the member of sales staff. It may even be a relationship breaker if repeated.

Argos, a major high street retailer with 316 stores across the United Kingdom, operates via a catalogue. This is now progressing towards interactive technology. At the end of 1993, Argos began to install a multi media catalogue on in-store terminals. Customers will be able to summon up on screen any item in the range by keying in codes from a series of menus. Having seen the item they wish, they are able to place an order knowing the piece is in stock. Based on ICL technology, the system arranges for the item to be available at a pick-up point. It updates inventories and is capable of creating a replenishment order on a supplier. Moreover, prices and ranges can be up to the instant.

Technology provides a way to overcome the pitfalls of its own change process. The route is a return to the historic concept of the market. It is Relationship Marketing.

I define Relationship Marketing thus:

Relationship Marketing is the consistent application of up-to-date knowledge of individual customers to product and service design which is communicated interactively, in order to develop a continuous and long term relationship, which is mutually beneficial.

In other words, marketing involves listening to consumers, interacting with them. It means establishing, recording and responding to their preferences. It implies appropriate and differentiated communications. Its end is a long-term relationship, whereby both the brand and the customer have the security of a relationship with the other. The reward is performance for the consumer, profit for the brand and peace of mind for both.

Figure 2.1, overleaf, demonstrates the process of marketing. It is a listening and learning exercise. Success depends on constant interaction between customer and vender. This interaction has a number of benefits for the organisation. Moving from an initial contact to a regular or irregular series of contacts provides a four-dimensional opportunity to the company, as Figure 2.2, overleaf, demonstrates.

Relationship Marketing embraces every form of market sector where repeat business is a part of the success formula. Even for funeral parlours, where there is a one-time purchase, a sensitive relationship may be built up with a particular family or community.

Relationship Marketing is the successor to **mass marketing**. The monologue of mass communication has given way to the dialogue of Relationship Marketing. The stages on the journey

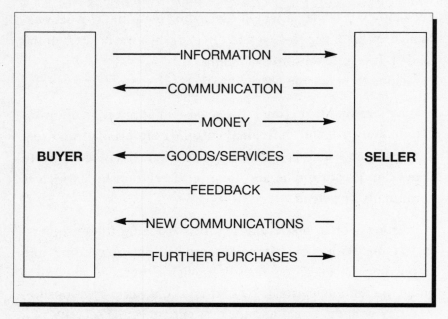

Fig 2.1 Marketing – an interactive process between buyer and seller

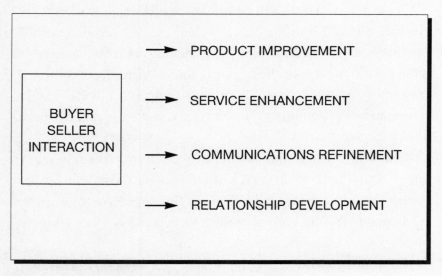

Fig 2.2 The benefits of interaction

have been flagged by marketing labels of the past decade and a half.

Database marketing was a key stage. This has been summarised as the ability of a direct marketer to address audiences as individuals despite their large numbers.

The concept of **maxi-marketing** has been described lucidly by Stan Rapp and Tom Collins, in their book published 1987, *Maxi-Marketing: The New Direction in Advertising, Promotion and Marketing Strategy*. This is the direct contact, dialogue and involvement with an individual prospect or customer leading to increased sales and brand loyalty.

In Summer 1990 Jonathon Copulsky and Michael J. Wolf of Booz Allen & Hamilton published their seminal article in the *Journal of Business Strategy*, entitled 'Relationship Marketing: Positioning for the Future.' In their view, Relationship Marketing combines elements of general advertising, sales promotion, public relations and direct marketing to create more effective and more efficient ways of reaching consumers across a family of related products and services. Their philosophy develops database marketing in consumer markets into share growth through technological skills.

Regis McKenna explored the concept further in his book *Relationship Marketing* (1991). He seeks to find a way to integrate the customer into the company, to create and sustain a relationship between the company and the customer.

Martin Christopher, Adrian Payne and David Ballantyne have focused on the dual task of getting and keeping customers. Their book 'Relationship Marketing' (1993) is subtitled, *Bringing Quality, Customer Service and Marketing Together*. Typically the mass approach has concentrated on bringing customers in, but has paid insufficient attention to retaining customers subsequently.

I now wish to expand the concept of Relationship Marketing, drawing from the historic routes of marketing, and describing the process with practical examples, guidance and recommendations.

Parallels between personal and commercial relationships

My theory is that a relationship between two individuals can be an analagy for the relationship between a firm or organisation and its customers. This applies to a consumer goods company, a firm in an industrial market, a local or a global service organisation. It also holds true for a charity in its relationship with its donors. The principles are the same.

To create the concept let us look at the example of communication. Communication is a critical part of any relationship. It applies equally to a relationship between a couple separated by geography, and the relationship between a brand and its consumers.

Successful personal communications . . .

Temporarily separated from a partner, one would keep in contact by exchanging letters and telephone calls with information and news to interest them. Messages could be sent via others. Photographs and mementoes could be provided and gifts given. Visits would be planned with special attention to the welcome greeting and the moment of parting. Finally, in a time of crisis, everything else would be put second in order to put matters right.

. . . and commercial communications

The same communication devices maintain a successful relationship with a remote customer. Direct mail to customers is a means of keeping in contact, provided that the information is personalised, relevant to the individual customer and well presented. It can be brief – sometimes a postcard can say all that is necessary. Care must be taken to ensure that the same letter is not sent twice or that people in the same household are not treated differently. Where a husband and wife have separate bank accounts, a letter to only one from the bank, making an offer or treating them as a more valued customer, can have repercussions! From the customer's viewpoint, all letters from the organisation contribute to the perception of the relationship – including invoices and reminders. All mailings need to reflect the desired impression of the relationship.

Inbound letters should be encouraged. A Freepost system can help here. Customer complaints, enquiries or comments need to be dealt with speedily, effectively and in a manner which is consistent with other forms of communication. Competitions are an incentive for customers to respond. Brands like Buitoni and Micro-Soft, companies like British Airways and Benetton have customer magazines featuring a deliberate series of invitations to correspond. Request a sample. Send in a recipe. Write a letter for publication. Take a photograph of the product in an unusual location. Suggest another way of using the product. Ask for a fact sheet or timetable. Every time that a customer writes to some part of the organisation, the relationship is further cemented.

Telemarketing is another form of keeping in touch with the customer. Ringing a person can feel intrusive if mishandled, but done well it can add real value to a relationship. Best use is in terms of an immediate and current offer. For example, it was used to great effect across Europe in the launch of both the Ford

Mondeo and Citroën Xantia to invite prospective buyers to a pre-view and test drive.

Making it easy for customers to ring the organisation is the other half of communication by telephone. In the USA, virtually all major packaged goods brands include a Careline number. In France 'numeros verts' are increasingly used. Fewer UK brands include 0800 numbers. Pioneers are brand leaders such as Coca Cola, Kelloggs, Flora, Batchelors, Timotei, Radion and Häagen-Dazs.

The benefits are clear. Any problem, query or concern can be raised and resolved in an instant. Potential opportunities for cross-selling may arise. Callers can be added to the data base and become a coterie of new product triallists. A mildly dissatisfied customer can be converted to a loyal user and advocate of the brand. Research by one of the largest UK banks indicated that customers who had had a problem resolved were 12 per cent more likely to take additional services than customers who had never made a complaint. People who care enough to ring up about a product are the most likely to spread praise or criticism in their social circles. Research cannot locate these opinion leaders, but they will identify themselves, given the opportunity.

Word of mouth marketing

This leads to the concept of 'Messages via others', or word of mouth marketing. A personal recommendation from an independent user counts for more than any other form of promotion. The recommendation may be implied by using the product in a social context. For example, an opinion leader may inspire others to drink Holsten Pils or Rolling Rock, wear Levi jeans or Nike trainers, and buy a Swatch watch. In other markets, advice seeking is traditional. Before buying a car, camera or CD system, most prospective purchasers would consult a colleague with experience. In corporate markets, executives would check with previous clients and users of computer systems, car lease services or accountancy practices. Some product users move from passive recommenders of their brand to confirmed advocates. Unprompted, they will promote the brand they use, in an appropriate context. Some newspapers and magazines engender this response – possibly because of the strength of relationship that they create with readers.

There are specific ways to encourage and enhance word-of-mouth marketing. These will be covered in Chapter 10.

What is a relationship?

The essence of the concept is that the relationships between an industrial company such as Bundy Tubing and its buyers like Rover, BMW, Opel and Skoda have fundamentally the same characteristics as are evident in the relationships between two individuals. The relationship between Mars and a consumer of M&Ms has a common basis. Donors and la Societe de la Croix Rouge share a bond.

There are some critical features in the relationships between two people. Let us look at these in turn and consider how they may be replicated in a commercial relationship.

A meeting

For an effective relationship to start, there has to be a meeting. At a party, this is a chance encounter. For a commercial relationship, there could be a meeting at an exhibition, a cold contact by phone or mail, or a reference by a third party known to both. In any event, there is a process of introduction – through another or on a one to one basis. There are initial impressions on which assumptions are made. It permits an instant form of evaluation. Is this person (or organisation) interesting, attractive or desirable as a partner? Do we work the same way? Are we potentially compatible? Are they on the same wavelength as me? For the relationship to progress to the next stage, it is necessary to have some positive answers to these questions.

A courtship

Phase two of a relationship is for there to be some sharing of information. This is a part of the 'getting to know you' process. The initial interest has developed into a relationship in its early stages. Like the courting process, there can be misunderstandings and misplaced assumptions which have to be straightened out if it is to continue. It is a period of trial and review. Expectations are created. They may be delivered or performance may fall short. Knowledge is gained through what is said and not said, what is done and what is not done. Gradually an understanding is formed of one by the other. Many relationships fail at this stage. For the bond to grow, both sides must value the understanding and wish it to continue.

Adjustments

The third phase is a subtle shift. It takes the form of an adjustment to each other. On an individual basis, some behavioural changes occur in response to the other party. These may be great or small. They may have a large impact or a minor one. The change may be imperceptible at first, but arise just the same. For a company, a new customer, however small scale, may make new requests, suggest new specifications, or come up with new levels of simplification or sophistication. A billion-pound corporation like Unilever will respond in some way to a new customer; for example, in its industrial fats business in Austria. The response will not be dramatic, or visible to a shareholder. Nevertheless if a particular baker supplied by the division would like a changed form of bulk packaging, the idea will be evaluated. The new idea may be adopted, or an alternative solution may be developed. In either circumstance, the baker has affected the corporation. A new relationship is a new stimulus. That stimulus may provoke change or encourage stasis, but it has an effect. The organisation learns. It is not the same.

Advancement

Different relationships grow at different rates. When it is possible for an individual to spend whole weeks together with a new partner, relationships can form, grow and develop rapidly. Where communication is less frequent and contact more restricted, then the time period may be greater. Communications are a critical feature of relationships. It is hard to sustain a relationship on a one sided basis. This is true for individuals and for companies. Regular two way communications build relationships. In the United States of America, the magazine *Seventeen* receives 6,000 letters every month from its teenage readers. Here is a demonstration of the reality of the relationship between reader and magazine. It shows how much trust they place in 'Seventeen'. Hamleys in London – one of the world's most famous toy stores – opened up a form of communication with its many hearing impaired customers. In conjunction with the National Deaf Children's Society, they had a signing Santa in the run up to Christmas. This is a dramatic illustration that communication is essential to relationships.

A mutual benefit

For a successful relationship between two individuals, it is normally necessary for each party to value the other in some way. This means that both parties see a benefit in the relationship. There is some give and take, some leeway, some mutuality. This is true in commercial relationships. For success, there is a need for both sides to appreciate the value of the other. It is a feature of both individual and commercial relationships, that one partner may need to remind the other of the value that they provide in the relationship! This may be done formally and directly, or alternatively, it may be suggested indirectly or implied.

There are personal relationships where one partner exploits or dominates the other. Likewise, these occur in commercial relationships. In both cases there are instabilities arising where threat, fear and control are significant elements. The underdog seeks an alternative, a form of escape, or simply acts passively in order to minimise the value to the dominant party.

Sincerity and integrity are normally pre-requisites for a good relationship. This applies equally to commercial or personal relationships. No one likes to feel they are being taken for granted. Insincere promises are deeply damaging to working relationships. Lack of confidentiality may lead to termination of a trading partnership. In essence, the virtues of trust and sincerity are as important in one to one personal relationships as they are to commercial agreements.

Despite all the indications of separations and divorces, the truth appears to be that people entering marriages believe in, or wish for a permanent relationship. They are thinking of the long term. It is not formalised as such in commercial relationships. A chief executive officer does not expect his purchasing director to place a lifetime contract with his suppliers. Ten year plans rarely break down future sales by customer, thus projecting relationships a decade hence. Yet the unspoken intention is that, all things being equal, we shall place our next order with our regular supplier. We are surprised when an order from a regular customer goes to another company. We act as if relationships will be long term. There is a parallel here between individual and commercial relationships.

For all these reasons I see a model for trading relationships in the way in which we like and expect our personal relationships to operate.

The polygamous corporation

Naturally, there are differences between a human relationship and a trading partnership between two corporations. No analogy can be followed slavishly. For example, polygamy is illegal in most countries. Yet a company, like Exxon can have a relationship with 500 million drivers, and more than a million commercial concerns. Perhaps, the need is not to be the only customer of Exxon, but to feel as if the service you receive at that moment is for you alone. In a relationship with one other, your uniqueness is appreciated. In a relationship that you share with a million other customers, your sense of individuality is at risk. The successful masters of Relationship Marketing realise this and create an individual bond with every customer.

SUMMARY

- There are three concepts in this chapter. Firstly, technology has provided a positive response to the chaos it began to create. Technology has given every person with responsibility for marketing the chance to extend a personal service to customers. It is not the personal service of the market stall of the

1790s. It is not the same attention as the frontier trader of the Far West gave his cowhand customers. But it has some of the elements of humanity that traders of those days relied upon.

- The mass culture, mass communications and mass marketing of the twentieth century have been an aberration from the norm. We are all individuals. Those who work for firms, companies, organisations, charities, collectives or partnerships see them as unique. For all these reasons we want and expect a service which recognises this.

- The technology that raised the mass market is now transforming it into a new individualisation. A customisation or tailoring process is occurring. Choice means that we can choose again to be individuals. We may choose to buy what our fellows buy, where they buy it and when they buy it. We may accept the same style of service as others, the same instructions for use or guidance and the same level of follow up. But that is our choice as buyers. Likewise it is the choice that our customers make as buyers of our products.

- Secondly, the consequence of this power of technology is that the style and nature of marketing are changing. The volume based marketing is being displaced by value based marketing. Relationship Marketing is coming to the fore. In essence, this is a sensitive and interactive form of marketing. It follows the development path created by database marketing. Using technology, Relationship Marketing works through individual understanding, design and communication to create long term, mutually beneficial relationships.

- Thirdly, the role model for the marketing of the next decade is the personal relationship. It may be the relationship between two individuals, or a market trader and his customer, or two corporations with a trading relationship, but the essence is the same. We are all individuals. We appreciate it when this is recognised.

- Success between now and 2005 will depend on harnessing technology, understanding Relationship Marketing and building the right relationships with the right customers.

3

THE VALUE OF RELATIONSHIP MARKETING

Long-term relationships have long-term benefits. These benefits have a value. The value may be financial, economic or social. Value differs according to different stakeholders of the organisation. Let us look first at the expectations of different stakeholders, and then consider how Relationship Marketing adds to the value created by an organisation.

An organisation has a range of individuals and bodies which look to it for some value.

Stakeholders

- The **shareholders, owners, or proprietors** will look for a return on their investment. Their expectation is likely to be consistency and certainty of profitability. Shareholders may be individuals, but more frequently are company pension funds and insurance companies, handling the investments of millions of people.

- **Employees and managers** will look to the organisation for income, probably security of employment, possibly training and development and ideally, job satisfaction. Employees and managers have families who depend wholly or partly upon them.

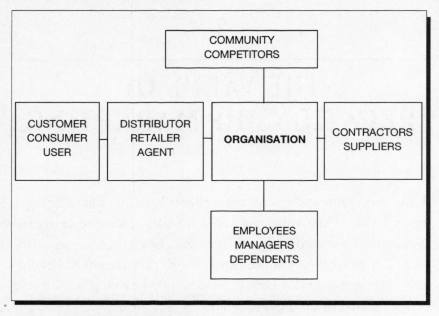

Fig. 3.1 The stakeholders of an organisation

- **Communities** also have a degree of dependency on organisations collectively. Local retailers may rely on the income
  from employees of major firms as the money circulates
  through their tills. The closure of a major employer like
  Zeveta in the Czech town of Bojkovice would have a domino
  effect on the whole level of trade and well being of the community.

- **Consumers, customers, retailers, distributors and agents**
  will look for product or service performance, image or range
  enhancement, continuity of supply and so on. The success of
  a dealer in construction equipment and diggers in Italy or
  Spain can depend significantly on the innovation and flair of
  J. C. Bamford, 2,000 miles away.

- **Suppliers, component producers, delivery organisations and service providers** will hope for continued and perhaps growing business, regularity of payment, ideas and suggestions for improvement, recommendations to other organisations, etc. Behind every customer order lies the supplier of the computer hardware, the designer and distributor of the accounting software, the manufacturer and wholesaler of the continuous stationery and the training company who briefed the staff on the systems.

- Even **competitors** may benefit from the value created by a rival. The rival may through innovation open up new market sectors for the industry. One shampoo manufacturer launches a clear variant, and all are free to learn from the concept. A rival may act to raise the status of the industry. The introduction of a state lottery may not jeopardise the business of a gaming concern, but actually expand the market. They may make the business more acceptable and fashionable. Of course, a rival may be a supplier of componentry in one division and a customer of a finished product in another.

- Other organisations in the not-for-profit also have the same variety of stakeholders. Charities for example, have beneficiaries, they have **donors, suppliers and servicing companies** as well as **employees.** Government departments exist in a system of the individuals or organisations who receive the service, employees, managers, the body politic and electors, as well as suppliers.

Depending on the organisation's strength

Every organisation, then, has a huge range of dependents. It is surrounded by stakeholders who all have an interest in its health and, normally, its long term survival.

Measuring that health

The current health of an organisation can be calibrated in various ways. Measurements include its annual profit, return on capital employed and, where the company is a publicly floated organisation, the share price. There are also trends shown by historical comparisons of these figures and current benchmarks.

$ £ FF DM

Financial measures are historical and current, and are unsafe predictors for the future. Steady profit growth in the past is no guarantee of a constant stream of future profits. A share price reflects future expectation, but often in an unscientific way which is clouded by other unrelated market events and prejudices.

Share %

Market share is another measure of organisational health, and one which may help forecast future organisational survival. Simply stated, a rising share is a positive sign, falling share is negative. There is much more to it than this. A deeper understanding of the quality of the market share itself, can indicate impending problems or prospective growth.

To understand the quality of market share, let us compare two mythical charities. They have been level pegging in terms of money raised for several years. Both generated the same income this year and so have the same share of the cake. They both receive 25 per cent of their income from legacies. The balance comes from donors: commercial and individual. In the first charity 80 per cent of the donors this year, also gave last year. The second charity raised the same amount in total, but only 50 per cent came from the people who had made donations in the previous year. Which charity is in the healthier position? Which charity is more likely to have the higher income in two years time? Which charity has the 'better' share?

'There's a hole in my bucket, dear Liza, dear Liza . . .'

The second charity is losing half its donors each year and having to recruit new ones to replace them. For a charity this is a serious concern. It means significantly higher administration costs. More computer records, more mailings, more appeals, more contacts, simply to raise the same revenue as the first charity.

'. . . a hole in my bucket, dear Liza, a hole!'

Two publishers of diaries have a consistent 20 per cent share of the business market, where diaries are bought in bulk by companies to give as gifts to customers. For publisher Number One, there is a significant degree of repeat business from companies who bought the previous year's diary. Let us say that his total sales are 100,000 units, of which 90,000 units are for current companies. For publisher Number Two, also selling 100,000 units, only 50,000 diaries are bought by existing customers. This means he has lost orders representing 50 per cent of last year's business. In a total market of 500,000 units, he has to find new orders for 50,000 diaries each year to stand still. Each year his sales team is seeking to capture 10 per cent of the market, to cover the 10 per cent lost.

A 'leaky' bucket needs topping up constantly

This leaky bucket syndrome is known as churning customers. This constant turnover of customers creates a number of major questions? For how many years can they do this successfully?

Where do all these customers come from? What happens when the market turns down and fewer new customers enter the market?

Durability of share

Durability of share is clearly important. The quality of market share may be defined as the proportion of your share which is repeat business. A high quality of share is where, relative to competitors, you have a greater proportion of sales derived from existing accounts, customers or clients. In rapid growth markets for new products or services, there is obviously less opportunity for high absolute percentages. As markets mature, those percentages will rise. It is therefore important to qualify the concept with a comparison versus competitors and the industry.

The automobile industry is very familiar with this concept. When the average repurchase rate for a marque in the United States of America was 40 per cent, Honda consistently achieved 65 per cent. Now Saturn is setting the pace. They have a higher quality of market share than most of their rivals.

How many customers are you losing?

The critical measurement behind the durability of market share is the attrition rate of customers. How many are lost each year? Typically, across most businesses in consumer and industrial markets, the average ranges between 15 per cent and 20 per cent.

An action point is to establish the attrition rate for your organisation. Do you know how many of last year's customers have failed to place an order this year? Is the figure reported and discussed at board level. Are trends monitored? Is the situation improving, or deteriorating? Are divisions, product groups or customer account teams monitored and compared? Do employees recognise it as a management priority?

Tracking your attrition rate is not a simple issue. It begins with the formal closure of an account. Your accounting system can identify these customers on a daily basis. It can also identify your established customers who have not ordered this week, month, quarter, half year or year. It can highlight each week lists of 'dawdlers' for the attention of account management.

Lost business is not necessarily announced. Transferring a checking account from one bank to another is so difficult, with so much effort required, that many dissatisfied customers discreetly open an account with a rival institution and progressively transfer their banking business over time. With slightly more sophistication, you can arrange for reports of 'decliners', who continue to use your service or place orders, but to a lesser extent which is below previous patterns. Human analysis is required to interpret trends and patterns.

Ideally the tracking system needs to have a level of expectation incorporated. How frequently is this customer likely to order? After what period without an order, should an investigation be made? What level of business shortfall should trigger a management report? These are all issues for investigation, debate and decision. Action can be taken to understand the attrition rate.

ACTION POINT CHECKLIST

- **Establish the attrition rate for your organisation.**

- **Do you know how many of last year's customers have failed to place an order this year?**

- **Is the figure reported at board level?**

- **Are trends in attrition monitored?**

- **Are divisions, product groups or customer account teams monitored and compared?**

- **Do your employees recognise it as a management priority?**

- **Does your customer tracking system include order cycle and value expectations in order to identify dawdlers and decliners?**

Measuring your attrition rate is the first step. Response must follow. The objective is to reduce the attrition rate. Although there will always be a level of attrition, from death, movement, company closure, structural change and new methods and practices, in most organisations there is considerable scope for bringing about a lower rate of customer loss.

Zero D means zero defections

Zero defects is a familiar target in manufacturing industry. 'Zero defections' is the target of customer management designed to minimise customer loss. Frederick F. Reichheld and W. Earl Sasser Jr have written persuasively on this theme in the *Harvard Business Review*. Frederick Reichheld is a vice president in the Boston office of Bain & Company and leader of the firm's customer retention practice. W. Earl Sasser is a professor at Harvard Business School.

Fewer defections = Higher profits

According to Reichheld and Sasser, companies can boost profits by almost 100 per cent just by retaining 5 per cent more of their customers. For instance, they draw attention to Charles Cawley, president of the Delaware based credit card company, MBNA America. Overwhelmed by letters of complaint from unhappy customers, he summoned all 300 employees of the company and declared that from now on they would satisfy and retain every single customer. The company began by collecting and analysing information from every defecting customer. They responded by amending processes, developing products and enhancing services appropriately.

As you would expect, quality improved. Fewer customers defected. Eight years later MBNA America's defection rate was one of the lowest in the industry. At 5 per cent, it was only half the average level for American credit card companies. Small percentage figures are misleading. In practice they result in enormous impacts on the bottom line. With only organic growth, MBNA America increased its profit sixteen fold, and moved from thirty-eighth most profitable in its industry, to fourth position.

This example illustrates the profit potential of better customer retention. It also demonstrates the methodology. It is the information that defecting customers pass on which is the key to success. Defecting customers are one of the best sources of market research available.

The truth comes out in exit interviews

Many bosses learn more about their style, shortcomings and bad practices from exit interviews than any annual employee appraisal meeting. Only when an employee is leaving does she or he feel free to tell the truth as they see it. The working relationship is over. There can be no fear of recriminations and no reason to hold back. There is no longer the potential compensation of further rewards. No need for sensitivity and subtlety. A complete and uncomplicated piece of feedback can be given.

There are emotional considerations in an employee exit inter-view. For example there may be elements of self justification and settling of old scores. However, when these are taken into account, an appraisal exists which can have real value. It can highlight issues which continuing employees dare not or prefer not to express.

Likewise, researching a customer who defects will provide a whole agenda of issues which current customers may not like to raise. Tactful and forgiving customers can mislead company researchers significantly. They may not want to hurt anyone's feelings, may not want to impugn their own judgement in using a poor quality service. They may balance a positive factor against a negative one and mention neither factor.

Defecting customers will give it straight. They will provide the sequence of events which caused them to go elsewhere. This can provide ideas for product and service improvements. It also provides priorities. For example, internally in many supermarkets accuracy of item pricing and billing may be seen as a priority. However, defecting customers may explain that accuracy levels are perfectly acceptable, it is the speed through the checkout that requires addressing. For servicing a heating, ventilation and air conditioning system, the time length in hours is less important, than the minimisation of disruption to employees and processes.

The big idea in defector research is that they will tell you which irritations they accept and which factor was the relationship breaker. You want to know, what makes people cease trading with you? What problem ended the business?

Surprisingly this type of research very often demonstrates that it is not what is done, but how it is done. The personal touch, the individual attention holds business. Its absence loses business. The sympathetic words 'You must be very annoyed about that, I will fix it immediately' can save relationships. In the same circumstances, the abrupt phrase, 'What do you expect me to do about that then?' could be the break point.

The lifetime value of the customer

This research illustrates the errors, shortcomings and faults that need to be rectified to retain more customers. Loyal customers have an enormous value, which customer management systems cannot record. Most accounting systems track the current costs as they are incurred. What they fail to show is the potential income stream from customers' future expenditure. The lifetime value of a customer can make an impressive total.

Imagine that every one of your personal customers is a millionaire. Most workers aged 25 today will certainly earn the equivalent of $1,000,000 in their working life and given some success and a slight inflationary trend, may exceed the equivalent of £1,000,000 by the time they retire. In industrial markets total revenues of corporations can amount to $ billions in only a small number of years.

To a news vendor in Manchester the customer buying every copy of *The Times* and the *Sunday Times* spends more than £10,000 in their lifetime. In its first year a new-born baby can soil $1,400 worth of single-use diapers. A medium-sized firm in Marseilles spending FF 16,000 per month on stationery and office supplies, will spend almost FF 2 million in a decade. Take your biggest customer and consider their total expenditure potential with your organisation in the next 15 years.

In one major US retailer, new staff members are taken to the front door of the store on their first day. The manager points out a young shopper entering and says 'you've just seen a hundred-thousand dollars walk in here!' It is a striking image. Thus a lost customer is not simply one lost sale. It is a chain of lost sales.

When a customer account is closed, a lifetime's income stream is closed off. There is a saying that it costs five times as much to recruit a new customer as it takes to retain one existing customer. I have never seen the research to support this statement, but intuitively it feels true. One study demonstrated that it cost 90 per cent of the annual gross margin of an average existing customer to cover the cost of capturing a new customer.

In financial services, most new cheque accounts are unprofitable for the first three years. In the UK, to attract 150,000 new student/youth accounts could cost £3,000,000 in advertising, and another £20 per head in incentives, mailings, literature, computer costs and administration. In early years, with high transaction levels and low balances, the business will be unprofitable. Profit comes with customer maturity, through higher income, higher balances, lending services, deposit products and insurance commissions. The proposition is only viable where the customer is retained.

Banks are all too familiar with the cost of customer recruitment. Many other organisations have no understanding of the costs per customer added to the account base.

The costs of winning a new customer

The costs come in obvious and less obvious ways. There are expenditures on advertising and direct mail aimed specifically at new users. This may require market research, buying in mailing lists of names and addresses, plus fulfilment services to respond to customers phoning or writing for more information. In industrial markets, it would be normal to allocate to new customers 40 per cent of the costs of hiring stands, manning and supporting exhibitions. Sales staff have a cost per hour, and designated time preparing, travelling to and presenting to potential accounts.

Wining and dining is expensive, but often necessary. Many directory advertisements are almost entirely for irregular and new purchasers. These are calculable costs extracted from the marketing budget. Senior management time and partner time may be directed to pitches in agencies and consultancies. These costs must be totalled and divided between the number of customers actually gained. In other words a 25 per cent strike rate will have twice the cost per customer as a 50 per cent strike rate.

Many organisations incentivise new customers with bonuses, gifts, or discounts. This is another cost to be added to the recruitment process. Some introductory discounts are difficult to phase out. There is also a contagious effect. Firstly the discount may become known to existing customers and aggravate them. Subscribers of *The Economist* are always finding special offer fliers slipping out of in-flight magazines. These bear a legend excluding them from benefiting. Longman Training have a video in their range entitled *Who Killed the Customer?* where this issue was the final straw in a collapsing commercial relationship.

The contagion may spread beyond your own customers. Price wars can be started by misreads of competitor pricing initiatives with new customers. Bob Garda and Mike Marn highlight this risk in an article in the *McKinsey Quarterly* 1993.

The costs of handling a new customer

Once the customer has accepted the proposition, there are all kinds of internal set-up costs. If it costs your company 30 DM to send a single letter, how much does a complete legal agreement cost? The procedure may include credit checks, account opening systems, staff briefings, new delivery instructions, new vehicle routing and packaging requirements. There could be hidden costs, such as reworking delivery notes when misprints occur, learning new contact numbers, coaching staff in slightly modified working practices. Handling new and unfamiliar customers actually takes longer than dealing with the known and regular accounts.

Charities too must take into account the cost of recruiting donors. These costs can easily inflate the all important administrative charges ratio. More sophisticated donors are rejecting charities where too high a percentage of revenue is consumed by administration. There is a vicious spiral whereby donor recruitment increases costs, ratios rise, donors drop off, income falls and ratios rise further.

Almost every company underestimates its costs of account set-up, and many ignore them in the wave of celebratory euphoria when a new customer is won. This does not mean that you should not attract new customers. It is a critical need to add to the account base to replace the genuine natural wastage of accounts, and to provide a contribution to growth. Nevertheless, for the mythical diary company replacing half its customer base each year, these costs are hidden drags on its profitability.

Habit as a barrier to recruitment

Another restraint on customer recruitment is the fact that human beings are frequently creatures of habit. We make choices and then often stay with these choices long after superior offers are available. Patterns are established, which rapidly become etched into us. In a research institute a mouse was placed in a maze. It had to find its way around barriers, over steps and through tunnels to the source of food. It accomplished this. Subsequently the mouse was placed in the same maze to find the food. Each time it was successful. Each time some barriers were moved to provide a shorter route. Every time it took the original longer path. Often human beings share this characteristic. Moving into a new apartment or house you take a decision to place the cutlery in a particular kitchen drawer. Even if you revise that decision the following day, you can still find yourself automatically reaching to the original drawer for a knife.

This theory of patterns implies that your potential customers are likely to be in a happy routine of buying from their existing suppliers. Of course, serious failures of product and service will loosen this tie. However the fact that people operate by patterns and approach change with some reluctance means that it is hard to take customers away from your rivals. This is particularly true of the most loyal type of customer. Existing customers are more likely to buy from you than people off the street. Existing customers of your rivals are more likely to buy from the rival than you.

It needs to be said that your potential customers are not waiting unserved in a product vacuum, listening attentively for your advertising message. They are locked in current arrangements, deaf to your blandishments. Prising customers away from your competitors is difficult. It is difficult when they provide a mediocre service. If they are excellent it is well nigh impossible. This stresses the value of existing customers and the importance of cementing that relationship for the long term.

In the long term, customers become increasingly profitable. There are a number of contributing factors to explain this. The example has already been cited of the bank customer who is effectively loss making in his or her first three years. They move into profit in year four and thus take perhaps six years to break even. After this they will be profit contributors to the bank.

Profit improvement over time

Frederick F. Reichheld and W. Earl Sasser Jr have provided an excellent framework to support this in an article entitled 'Zero Defection: Quality Comes to Service'. It appears in the *Harvard Business Review* of September–October 1990. Their studies of 100 companies in two dozen industries illustrate a consistent pattern of improving profitability over time.

Acquisition costs impact on the first year profitability. Reichheld estimates that for a credit card company the first year loss is $51. All the costs described in paragraphs above will reduce the first year profit. After these costs are covered, the customer transactions bring a base profit. This is the normal trading margin with which you will be familiar.

Over and above this base profit, there are additional benefits. Over time customers tend to purchase more from you. Initially they are experimenting, trying out your service. Purchases will be evaluated. Satisfaction will be shown in higher levels of purchase. A retail shopper pleased with a blouse may return and buy a second blouse, but this time she may take a scarf as well. The window-cleaning contract for an office block has been carried out successfully, so for the subsequent year a second building may be added to the arrangement, or negotiations open on an interior cleaning contract with another division of the contractor.

Banks call this process cross-selling and aim to increase the customer's holding of other products across the range. Purchasing directors call it 'rewarding reliability', and they endeavour to place further business with concerns who will deliver expectations. Single sourcing of components by Nissan in their manufacturing plant on Tyneside in the north east of England is a measure of the importance of reliability in supply.

The incremental additions of services, or increasing purchase of goods across the range comes with greater confidence and trust. It occurs naturally as familiarity with individuals increases. The longer the relationship, the better the sales people understand the customer and the more opportunities the customer receives to find out about extra services available from the supplier. For one industrial distributor, research found that net sales per account were continuing to rise into the 19th year of the relationship. Thus profit grows from the increasing volume of purchases.

Profit also grows from the reduction in operating costs. This is often not captured by conventional accounting systems. New customers do not understand the service, the supplying organisation, or the language. It takes time and resource to educate them, so that they are familiar with methods and procedures. The first time a customer enters a Burger King, they have to learn what a 'Whopper' is. They may even ask to have it described, or wish to know whether it contains onion. This takes staff time. On a subsequent visit, this explanation will be unnecessary.

When a leasing company begins to provide the fleet vehicles for a company, there will be a host of telephone enquiries about procedures. In the first week of the contract, there could be dozens of calls covering issues like windscreen damage, punctures, approved servicing outlets, self repair and insurance cover technicalities. In the second week, the number of calls will diminish, and this level of service requirement will decrease progressively until a minimal support is needed. This may take two to three years to bring about. However if you measure the support level against the time length of customer relationship, there is a strong correlation.

Errors arise in unfamiliar areas. New customers make mistakes. They complete order forms incorrectly. They misunderstand 'Units of Issue' and order ten when they need one hundred. Likewise, the supplier will not know the intricacies of the new business and make errors themselves. Rectifying these is expensive. These costs are usually camouflaged in telephone bills, carriage costs and employee overtime. With time the expanding mutual knowledge means mistakes arise very much less often. Costs are lower.

There is also an experience curve effect. As the relationship extends, cost savings occur. It is normal for these to accrue in the main to the supplier to boost his margin. This is not always the case. Recent contracts from Toyota provide for single source supply, but stipulate a lower cost in year two and a further reduction in unit price in year three. This is based on the sharing of benefits of the experience curve.

There is another level of profit benefit. The longer a relationship continues, the greater the likelihood of business referrals. Long term customers become, in effect, an extension of your own sales team. Their word also has a far greater worth than the spiel of a paid salesman.

The referral may be passive where you simply mention that you have been supplying the buyer in question for 25 years. This is a form of implied endorsement. You may actually suggest that the potential buyer approaches some of your long-term customers for a reference. The customers may spontaneously recommend your service or product to their peers and contacts. Word-of-mouth advertising is the most powerful form of persuasion available in industrial markets.

Finally, long-term customers often pay a premium for service. They know that they could go out into the market and obtain a lower cost. There is however a value to them in the relationship in which they have confidence. There is the certainty of switching costs for the customer. New arrangements, training and set-up costs are a real penalty for switching suppliers. And the current supplier service fits them like a glove – it has been tailored to them over the years. There is a 'FUD' factor in change –

fear, uncertainty and doubt. Every young buyer is aware of the career damage threat of a switch from an established reliable supplier to a cheaper but unproven rival. For all these reasons the long term customer can be paying a price premium.

Taking all these elements of profit into account, it can be seen that long term customers are substantially more profitable than new accounts. This is true in consumer markets and industrial markets, in Canada and Korea, for products and services.

SUMMARY

- Long-term relationships pay. Short-term relationships are expensive. There are huge penalties, visible and hidden, for companies who churn their customers. For companies who keep customers over the decades, the value is enormous. Relationship Marketing is about creating, nurturing and maintaining successful long-term relationships. In conclusion, value comes from managing relationships well. This value is delivered to all the stakeholders who depend directly or indirectly on the health and survival of the organisation.

4

MAKING IT HAPPEN

Ensuring the health and survival of the organisation is a responsibility that the organisation owes to its stakeholders. Being in business means a commitment to those whose lives and livelihoods the enterprise affects. It means delivering the implicit promises to employees, managers and their dependents, shareholders, pensioners, suppliers, customers, service companies and distributors. Running an organisation is keeping a series of commitments to those stakeholders. The only route to health and the long term survival of the organisation is through managing relationships. To make it happen, you need to make Relationship Marketing happen.

How do you bring Relationship Marketing into being in your organisation?

You need a system for recruiting and retaining customers for the long term. You need an interactive process, which means that your organisation is able to learn from its experiences. This learning enhances the range of products and services. The interactions also mean that progressively, stronger relationships are built up. It seems elementary and simple.

Most of the concepts on which Relationship Marketing is based are simple. People agree with them naturally. They are not contentious. Most organisations understand some of the mechanics. They have elements in place. They are aware of some aspects. However it is necessary to put the whole jigsaw in place to receive the whole benefit. There is a synergy from the different factors. Each element supports and reinforces the others to deliver a total performance.

This handbook aims to explain the steps necessary to achieve the potential of relationship marketing.

It will permit organisations to audit where they currently stand. They can identify the gaps in their effectiveness and take the measures to remedy and improve the situation.

A journey, not a destination

You never end up as a perfect organisation. Life is not like that. The experience of well-researched books on excellence is that it is a time based phenomenon. In other words a firm can be excellent according to the conditions of the time. And just as management feel they understand their environment, it changes. Just as they feel they know which levers to pull to achieve the desired result, the levers change. We live in a mobile, changing, metamorphosing world. Everything changes, but all at different rates.

The cardinal virtue of organisations in the 1990s is agility. It is the ability to respond smoothly, flexibly and rapidly to new circumstances. Relationship Marketing is not a one-off solution for a space in time. It is an approach to business that means responding to a developing understanding of a moving landscape.

Relationship Marketing in practice

To see how the theory operates in reality, let us first step back in time to picture the tradesman of 200 years ago. Let us imagine he has a successful business in his market town.

As his business grew, he would need extra help. He would

need more hands. It was not possible to do everything himself. For him, new hands started as apprentices. They would begin at the bottom of the business. The tradesman would chose his apprentices carefully. Probably he had watched them grow up from childhood and knew their families. Selecting them was a deliberate and careful matter. He would be investing a great deal in them. He would expect them to be with him for a long time. In his absence, they were the sole representatives of his business. His good name depended on them.

Let us consider his approach to business. He welcomed the opportunity to sell his wares, but not indiscriminately. Perhaps there were some customers he chose not to deal with. Maybe they did not have good credit, possibly because of past dealings or misdemeanours they had unworthy names. A man's reputation was affected by the people he mixed with. Perhaps they were simply too much trouble to deal with. Or they flitted from one supplier to another.

Having chosen those who he wished to trade with, he got to know these people well. He invested time in talking to and listening to them. He discovered their likes and dislikes, their circumstances, the things happening in their lives. He changed as they changed. In fact, he knew them so well, he almost knew what they wanted, before they knew themselves. He always seemed to know what was coming into fashion. He kept in touch with his customers. They were never forgotten. He kept his promises to them. He used his knowledge of his customers and their changing needs to keep his staff up-to-date, so that they were always ready to serve them. He shared his knowledge.

Lastly, he kept an eye on the whole of the business. He remembered where he had come from, knew where he was at the moment, and sensed where he was going. He kept track of the money coming in and flowing out. He kept his commitments in mind.

He may not have been aware, consciously of carrying out all these steps. They occurred naturally. They also occurred simultaneously, rather than in a particular sequence.

Keeping a business in step

Yesterday's tradesman had one advantage over today's business leaders. He could keep his whole enterprise in his mind's eye at one time. He was not a prisoner of scale. As a result of this, the whole organisation moved in step. It was as consistent as if the whole business was a person. His business was an extension of himself. He had a personality, his business shared it, or was a further reflection of it. To achieve this today is very much more challenging.

Looking at how he ran his operation, there are some valuable guidelines to a modern business. They are not rules, but guidelines to making a large scale business reflect the individual virtues of a person. They are steps on a journey. The terrain, weather and conditions change, but the principles of Relationship Marketing will serve the traveller in staying in touch with his or her business.

I describe seven steps. This is for the purpose of understanding and to permit an audit of current performance to establish priorities. The steps are actually linked. They are parallel activities, feeding back and reinforcing each other.

Seven steps

The seven steps are as follows:

1 You need loyal staff. Calibrate and raise the level of loyalty of staff. Loyal staff create the organisational efficiency and understanding to achieve the retention of customers. Without

the support of loyal staff you cannot succeed. Chapter 5 describes this step.

2 You need loyal customers. Choose the customers who are likely to be loyal. Some segments of customers are inherently disloyal. Spot the butterflies and let them flit between your competitors. Chapter 6 describes this step.

3 You need to know your customers well. Ensure you have accurate, relevant and meaningful data. You must change with your customers. They will change, grow and develop. Learn where and how to change. Which way is the market heading? Know about change first. Be fastest to respond. Chapter 7 describes this step.

4 You need to price appropriately. You must understand your opportunities and constraints. How do you handle falling real prices? How do you keep faith with long term customers? Relationship pricing. Chapter 8 describes this step.

5 You must communicate with your customers. Keep in touch. Keep listening. They are individuals, so personalise your communications and make them interactive. Be consistent and reliable. Chapters 9 and 10 describe this step.

6 You must upgrade your staff constantly. Set the standards and equip the staff to deliver those standards. Coach them, train them, update them, encourage them. Chapter 11 describes this step.

7 You must hold it all together. Keep the organisation in step. Keep in control and keep the relationship flourishing. Chapter 12 describes this step.

These steps are now described in detail, chapter by chapter.

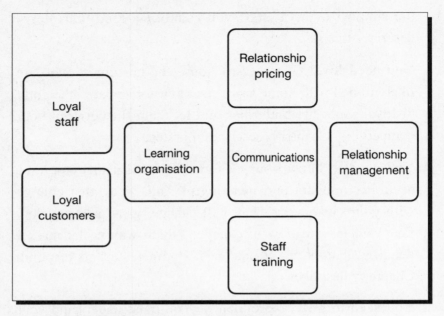

Fig 4.1 Relationship marketing – the seven steps

So how do you make it happen?

This chapter is entitled 'Making it Happen'. So how do you make it happen? My suggestion is that you involve three people to read each chapter. They should be interested parties, with a shared understanding of the organisation's objectives. Having read a chapter, they should carry out a **SAW** ANALYSIS. Individually they should assess the **STRONG POINTS – AVERAGE POINTS – WEAK POINTS** of your organisation in terms of the recommendations of that chapter.

- **Strong points.** Highlight the aspects where you are particularly strong. The key issue here is to consider how can you maintain and build that strength.

- **Average points.** Then look at aspects where you are no

worse than anyone else. You are at industry standard. Which dimensions will make a discernable difference? Which are the order winning criteria? Which are the bonding mechanisms? Prioritise for action.

- **Weak points.** Next, look at areas where you know you are weak. Produce a priority list for rectification.

Having carried out an individual assessment, the three people should discuss their separate analyses to determine a consensus position. Collectively, what do they feel are the key actions necessary to enhance your corporate performance on that dimension of Relationship Marketing?

Implementation follows agreement in principle. For some strategic aspects you will wish to act in an executive capacity. In most areas, you will wish to consult with staff involved to confirm acceptance and gain further contributions. For most issues, your strategy will be to share the problem or concern with the team and encourage them to determine and take the action.

General George S. Patton said, *'Never tell people how to do things. Tell them what you want them to achieve, and they will surprise you with their ingenuity'*.

You are providing strategic direction, not specific directions. The team will make Relationship Marketing work.

Relationship Marketing is a long-term philosophy. It is a continuing approach to business, rather than a quick fix. Therefore, you will want to ensure that you revisit the concept regularly. Actions need to be built into the way of life, measured and managed.

Milestones

We have described Relationship Marketing as a journey, not a destination. To follow this allusion a little more, 'milestones' are essential. In other words, you need time based measurements of performance or improvement. They point out the way and where you wish to be by a certain time. For example, within three months from now, 50 per cent of order handling staff will have spent a day at the premises of a major customer. Milestones are a form of confirmation of policy to the team, and a valuable measure of whether you have travelled far enough in the time. The most effective milestones are those created by teams themselves, subject to your overseeing that they are not overstretching. Of course all milestones will need to reviewed and revised from time to time.

SUMMARY

- This book is designed as a workbook. Practical guidance is provided for you to identify the areas for focus for your organisation. Its aim is to help you to keep your organisation fit, healthy and, above all, agile so that it may respond to the changes and opportunities technology is constantly creating.

5

LOYAL STAFF

Putting Relationship Marketing into practice begins with the staff in your organisation. It is impossible to create a long, happy and loyal relationship with customers and clients if you do not have loyal and well-motivated staff. This chapter explores the idea of creating and maintaining loyal staff as a first step to Relationship Marketing.

'It all starts with loyal staff'

Loyal staff are the first point in the concept of the creation of an effective enterprise. It can be expressed very simply. If you want happy shareholders, you need happy customers. If you want happy customers, you need happy staff. It does not work in reverse.

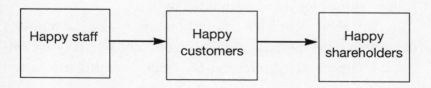

This sequence of dependent priorities is very evident in airlines. Jan Carlson, in revitalising the airline SAS, began with the staff. He took over at the low point of their financial crisis. Immediately one of his first acts was to hold vast meetings of the staff in the aircraft hangars. Without their understanding and support, he could achieve nothing. Together, they made punctuality possible. They collectively ensured that planes were scrupulously clean. They smiled and set passengers at their ease. Airline passengers are not human cargo – they are individuals with hopes, fears, likes, dislikes, moods and needs. Human beings need the human service that only fellow humans can provide. A service industry depends on the knowledge, interest, commitment, verve and enthusiasm of the people providing the service.

It is not just service industry companies that depend on their staff to humanise their approach. A charity will operate in the same way. The people demonstrate the commitment which makes the donors give. The credibility of the charity relies on every member of its team, voluntary and salaried.

Manufacturing industry too, relies on its service providers. Increasingly it is becoming true of all industries that the service element forms the differentiation for success. As manufactured items from competing organisations converge in design, technology and attributes, it is the service aspect which makes one car, one mobile telephone or one office carpet seem different and better than another. For a manufacturer to deliver the expectations he has set up, he needs people to make it happen. These people must be loyal and committed staff.

In the public sector, government operations and the military, the picture is the same. In his book on the Gulf War, *Storm Command* (HarperCollins), General Sir Peter de la Billiere wrote:

In the end, success depended on individuals, whether they were pilots, divers, tank drivers, mechanics, engineers, cooks, radio operators, infantrymen, nurses, or officers of all ranks. It was these ordinary people who, at the end of the day, were going to put their

lives on the line, and risk their necks when their government decided to go to war.

Success does indeed depend on each of the individuals supporting their team in the enterprise.

Why staff loyalty is critical

We looked at the costs of customer churning earlier. We saw that
there are obvious costs and concealed costs from a constant
outflow and inflow of customers. The most profitable organisations keep costs down through keeping customers who are familiar with the systems and procedures, require less support and
appreciate the relationship. Exactly the same principle applies to
staff.

Let us begin with recruitment. Recruiting staff is an expensive
and time-consuming activity. Time is taken to agree a need for a
recruitment. Approval may be necessary, so that there is a
requirement for a justification. To determine a salary or wage, a
grade may be needed, which might require a grading panel to be
convened. When the decision is made and confirmed an advertisement is frequently the next stage – in a local, national or international publication. The advertisement will reflect badly on
your corporate identity if it is not professionally laid out and
designed. Perhaps you believe that 'Big companies cannot use
small ads', which increases the cost. During the recession in
Canada and Germany, a job advertisement could attract hundreds
of replies, in some cases even thousands. Sorting through an
application at one per minute can easily take half a day. Alternatively you may use an executive search agency. This will take
time in the briefing and could cost as much as 30 per cent of the
annual salary plus expenses. Even for very junior positions, it is

possible to be overwhelmed with applicants, so that it is hard to identify the prime candidates from the 'also rans'.

Interviewing is the conventional approach to assessing suitability for employment. To see even four candidates only once can occupy a whole day. The time between interviews is rarely productive, as the manager is trying to hold the memory of the comparative attributes until the next interview. Many interviews involve two or even three managers. Perhaps psychological assessment or ability testing is deemed necessary. References need to be taken. There may be legal and insurance procedures.

Having recruited the new employee, training comes into play. This can take management time to devise, arrange and conduct. There are costs and disruptions to raise the recruit to proficiency, and to familiarise them with people, procedures and practices. In the early days of a position, there can be down-time from lack of familiarity, misunderstandings and mistakes. The philosophy of giving staff 'freedom to fail' is a marvellous learning tool – we learn more from our mistakes than any other way, and corrected mistakes change behaviour patterns. However, too many people who are free to fail in too short a time can play havoc with customer relationships. One person learning and making a mistake is tolerable. TSB Bank put notices on the serving windows of new tellers, asking for patience while a new team member gains experience. Customers welcome this new blood with warmth and optimism. However a branch with four teller positions, three of which bore such a notice, would be unacceptable.

New staff are not familiar with the shortcuts available to carry out their roles speedily. They have to find out that they do not need to call up the file option on their screen and follow the full procedure, but instead they can quickly click on to the file icon. Until customer telephone numbers are committed to memory, they need to be sought on screen or in a directory. An enquiry from a customer or a colleague has not arisen previously, so an instant response cannot be provided. New staff are constantly inefficient through this learning experience.

Existing staff have their own efficiency lowered by being trainers and rectifiers. This can affect morale and commitment.

Staff leaving after, say, a year may never have operated efficiently for you. This is true at junior and senior levels. Churning staff secretly consumes company time, company money and company commitment. The costs are rarely shown in the accounts or in inter-company efficiency comparisons. Yet they are very real.

Benefits of staff continuity

There are six benefits of staff continuity:

- Role familiarity

- Colleague familiarity

- Product familiarity

- Customer familiarity

- Culture familiarity

- Contribution

Being familiar with the role

Firstly, there is role familiarity. Whilst many positions in small and large organisations have job descriptions, these do not truly provide a pattern for behaviour in the role. Only experience can do this. Thorough understanding of the responsibilities and requirements of a post comes only from the inside. Excellent delivery drivers, copy-writers, plant managers and finance vice presidents are the product of time in position. The genius on Day One is a myth! Every job has its learning curve, and you benefit when most people are some way down that curve.

Knowing the colleagues and their characteristics

Secondly, there is colleague familiarity. An organisation is a collection of individuals, each of whom has their special skills and abilities, their personal weaknesses and foibles. Over time a new team member comes to know these strengths and weaknesses through experience. He or she knows who to consult for a particular case. On whom can you rely? Who needs chasing for progress? Whose advice will be better for a delivery to a new Australian customer? Who is risk averse and who is thrill driven? Frequently football clubs seem to play with greater fluidity and flair than national sides. Perhaps this may be because the regular team consists of players who know each other day in day out, in good and bad situations, working and relaxing. The national team comprises players who will have trained together, but cannot know each other as well as a club side. You benefit when your team know each other well enough to play harmoniously together.

Really knowing the product and service

The third benefit is product familiarity. By product, I include service, support and structure. The longer an employee has been with a firm, the greater is the depth of product knowledge. The experienced test pilots at Boeing in Seattle will have focused on virtually every component affecting a planes's performance during their careers. The feel of a plane and the way it handles comes from hundreds of contributing elements. That is product familiarity. The mature salesman at Pakistan's English Biscuit Company will know every question about the taste, recipes, packaging, shelf life, delivery of the biscuits, and a variety of answers, from the simple and reassuring to the sophisticated and scientific.

The huge benefit from product familiarity is the confidence it brings with it. Imagine that you are called in to see your boss and asked a question. If your answer uses up your complete knowledge of the particular subject and you know that any follow-up question will baffle you, then you are unlikely to sound totally confident. On the other hand, if that answer is 1 per cent of your knowledge and you cannot conceive of a follow-up question that you cannot address, you will probably radiate confidence. The confidence is not in the words alone, but in the bearing, composure and attitude. Putting sales and support staff in front of customers with this confidence requires a depth of knowledge that only comes from experience. You benefit when your staff have that confidence.

Knowing your customers

The fourth benefit is customer knowledge. Over time every one gathers a knowledge of regular and long term customers. This may be at first hand, or it can be indirectly though others in the organisation. Staff begin to be able to predict customer responses to situations based on previous experience. Which accounts will react to what. Who will see the funny side of a situation and who will never take a joke. Which clients contribute good ideas to a new project and which prefer to be presented with the final version only. An undocumented understanding of customer needs, expectations and standards develops. It is undocumented because it grows, develops and changes on a weekly basis. Of course, the familiarity with a customer is really with individuals in a customer organisation, but the behaviour of these individuals reflects the consistency of a corporate culture. If the behaviours of key players in a customer are stochastic, then that inconsistency is another piece of knowledge. Your customers benefit from this understanding and empathy, and you benefit from their appreciation.

Culture keeps your company together

The fifth benefit continues the idea of the culture of an organisation. This time, it is the culture of your organisation. You cannot manage every decision or situation involving an employee. You would not wish this. Yet you need and expect a certain style and approach to be adopted in every decision and situation. A book of rules and procedures is not the answer. The right answer is the role model, and the culture. You act as role model for your team. You demonstrate the way 'things are done around here', in person and by the rewards and recognition to others following this pattern. Gradually this accumulated body of staff example and experience begins to form a culture. It is the behavioural cement that binds an organisation together in its endeavour.

New staff take some time to assimilate and understand the 'Shell way', the quick and clear approach at Jardine Pacific Ltd, the 'Sheraton standard' or the 'manière de Credit Suisse'. They learn by observing, by testing and through their corrected transgressions. A familiarity with the company culture helps to maintain consistency in the organisation. Staff partially set their own expectations and become self managing. This develops that culture and supports its continuity and adaptation. On the other hand, a constant inflow of new staff is a challenge to a culture.

You benefit when the culture reinforces the values you espouse and the staff behaviours are in keeping.

Contributions which add value

The sixth benefit flows from the other five. If employees are familiar with their role, each other, the product portfolio, customers and the company culture, they can make a far greater contribution. Each employee has a common framework for adding value to his or her efforts. Ideas, improvements, inspirations are more likely to be matched to the organisational competence and customer needs, if these familiarities exist. You benefit from the efficiency of product, service and customer development.

Health warning!

These then are six positive and valuable benefits of staff loyalty. They have been stated in the context of being desirable attributes. They are stated in this form because most organisations in Europe, the Americas, Australia, Hong Kong, South Africa and New Zealand change their staff too frequently. Not all fall into this category. Some retain a stultifying rejection of any new blood. New people, ideas, approaches are constantly needed. Without inventors, mavericks and radical thinkers, organisations fossilise in their thinking and decline. There is some middle ground between the corporate style of a dinosaur and the New York Stock Exchange. My view is that the balance has swung to much towards treating employees like shares to be traded, not assets to be polished and valued. An action point is for you to consider your approach to employees.

You probably need to review the benefits listed above, and consider how better to capture those benefits.

A menu for staff loyalty, not a recipe

This set of action points is a menu not a recipe. There is no single recipe for achieving staff loyalty. There are a variety of ideas, suggestions, recommendations and model approaches. Look at this series of possibilities, audit yourself and make an action plan to address the weaknesses and enhance the strengths you see in your organisation.

Strategy development has three phases. These are shown in Figure 5.1.

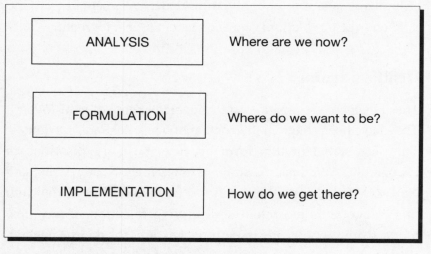

Fig 5.1 Strategy development – three stages

A strategy for staff loyalty

The strategy for achieving staff loyalty takes the above form. Each point is considered in sequence, beginning with analysis as Stage One.

Analysis

You begin by determining the current status. This requires careful definition of parameters before you begin the analysis. What exactly are your success criteria? How do you define the level of current performance? What are your sources of information? How do you evaluate them?

The entry point is that you are aiming to achieve three dimensions. Firstly, you wish to recruit the right candidates who are able to perform the tasks designated to your standards. Secondly you wish to retain these individuals. Thirdly, you aim for a well motivated team with a positive and supportive esprit-de-corps.

For each of these dimensions, you need to have a proxy measure, or set of measures to calibrate your standing. This seems almost pseudo-scientific because much depends on personal assessment and is inherently subjective. So be it. You cannot remove subjectivity from business in the short run. In the long term, it must become nearer to objective or the standard perishes.

Recruiting – Are we good enough at it?

For the first measure, you might wish to establish a four- or six-point scale to be completed by the manager, and/or an independent manager, and/or a team member. The assessment would take place three months to nine months after recruitment, judging how far the new recruit met the standards set at the outset. The scale is better run on four or six dimensions, as the temptation on a scale of one to five is to place most candidates in the average level of three. An even number of options forces a choice between 'good' and 'bad'. Further assessments can take place regularly with an appraisal cycle or at the anniversaries of appointment. Checks and measures will establish 'How effective are we at finding and attracting the right people?'

Can we keep them?

For the second measure, you are simply measuring retention. What proportion of people recruited are still in position after six months, one year, eighteen months, two years, three years? It is an absolute figure or percentage. However, there is then the sub division of the figures. Retention can be measured by department, division and company. It can be analysed by recruitment source. For example, what is the retention by age at recruitment, and by qualification. Are recruits with Masters degrees in Business Administration really more mobile than staff recruited straight from school? Are new staff bought in from rivals in your industry likely to stay or move on?

The exit interview tells all

The analysis needs to encompass a comprehensive exit interview. Just as I suggested you consult defecting customers to learn about your organisation, so you can learn from defecting employees. The major and minor reasons for leaving should be recorded. They can give an indicator to future recruitment practice or motivations.

Motivation?

The third dimension is the level of positive motivation of staff. This has to be a challenge to measure. In some ways it is the most subjective area. Yet walking into a department where morale is low is a near tangible experience. The contrast with the buzz of a well-motivated team is very obvious. In small organisations you have to feel the atmosphere, to sense the mood and to gauge the issues which need addressing. The same is true of larger businesses. However, a more structured approach can support 'management by walking about'.

Rank Xerox, who have an enviably low staff turnover ratio, conduct regular staff satisfaction surveys. These monitor employee opinions and attitudes across 101 statements. The statements are derived from in-depth discussion with staff at every level, on all the issues which may concern people. The issues range from physical matters like heating and lighting, through colleagues and co-operation levels, to topics like perception of quality and confidence in the organisation for the future. Staff are able to grade their response according to agreement/tend to agree/unsure/tend to disagree/disagree. These comprehensive surveys indicate where the organisation now stands as far as employees are concerned. They also identify the root causes of dissatisfaction for priority redress.

It is well appreciated that this form of exercise is in parallel with frequent personal contact, and is no substitute for first-class boss/subordinate relationships. Continuing surveys are better than one-off 'Grief and Aggro' studies. There is a danger in a single survey, which simply implies that this was a temporary management fad, and is not a commitment to a long-term understanding of changing attitudes.

The data gathered can show trends, directions and suggest actions only if there are comparators. I suggest that there are several options for comparison. The trend over time gives a developing picture. This applies particularly to retention levels and employee satisfaction. Comparison between yourself and other companies is useful, when possible. Locally a plant can share data on staff retention with neighbouring and non-competing firms through chambers of trade and other business community organisations. Trade associations often permit you to share information within an industry if the information is seen to be nonconfidential. Finally, there is an opportunity to use this as a dimension of a bench-marking exercise with an agreed partner.

Formulation

What is your ideal? Using the information you have gleaned from the measurements of your current status, it is possible to set objectives for each of the elements. Which types of recruitment tend to be the most successful? You can set targets for the sort of people to attract. You can aim for the level of staff turnover appropriate to your business.

But the world is in turmoil . . .

All this takes place in a world where takeovers are rife, where bankruptcies threaten your suppliers, customers and rivals, where out-sourcing of production processes is always under review, where contracting out of services is often a next stage. These pressures are true. They are not, however, reasons why you should not strive to set targets for recruiting the best staff, retaining them and keeping them motivated. The challenge of the environment means that you have an opportunity to distance yourself further from your competitors if you can get it right. In Hong Kong, where job mobility is legendary, organisations which can hold core staff longer than rivals gain a real competitive advantage.

The reality is that employees know and understand the challenges as well as you do. They appreciate that there are no guarantees of life long organisational stability. What is valued is the approach from you which says you are doing the very best you can to create long-term employment. Thus, if you choose to contract out work, the objective would be that the new contractor takes on existing staff. Where roles change, endeavour to foresee and retrain staff involved. Circumstances will sometimes allow you to work in this way and sometimes thwart these intentions. Trust is inspired through commitment openly to doing your best. Share your aims and your legitimate concerns.

Implementation

The third stage of the strategy development process is the implementation. The best ideas for implementation always come from inside an organisation. When the current situation is measured and understood and you have set aims, there is a gap. That gap is a stimulus to you and your team to construct actions which close that gap. For example, to minimise staff turnover, you need first to know why staff are leaving, which issues could and should be addressed. It is then possible to look in turn at the problems and develop company solutions.

An idea bank

There are a number of ideas which may act as thought starters for you to develop your own solutions. These ideas are structured in sequence: Who do you recruit? Where do you find them? How do you manage it? How do you retain people?

Recruiting staff

Relationship Marketing offers and expects long term loyalty from staff, suppliers and customers. Recruiting means attracting individuals who share these approaches in their lives. Service is a critical part of Relationship Marketing. The new people you seek must be conscientious in their service to colleagues, suppliers and customers.

Quality has come out of the inspection department and is now the province of every employee. Therefore you need individuals who care passionately for the quality of their own performance.

Thirdly, the pace of change facing your organnisation places a priority on recruiting people who will cope well with this new and uncertain environment. This suggests searching for people who also display adaptability. Ask for a willingness and ability to learn. Check for a personality which can cope with uncertainty.

Service orientation, commitment to quality and adaptability – these precepts have applied to executive positions. They now apply to all positions. Technical aptitude and qualifications become hygiene factors which are noticeable only in their absence. The critical factors for choosing between two entry level candidates move to the dimensions of the senior executive.

Two ideas to challenge you

You specify age in your advertisements. There is an upper limit. Why? If you are looking for staff with an ability to cope with uncertainty, why not recruit from an age group who have tasted it? If you want service orientation, loyalty and a concern for quality, maybe you should seek older staff who offer these characteristics. Open up to the possibility that the old rules are wrong rules. If you automatically rule out older recruits, examine your prejudices. They may actually take less sick leave than their younger and ostensibly healthier counterparts. Are they really incapable of operating the user friendly computer terminals you have at the work stations? Think again.

B & Q are a British chain operating over a hundred do it yourself stores, offering a huge variety of tools, paints, electrical equipment, plumbing, bricks, tiles, cement, wood and so on, in large out-of-town retail parks. Their big challenge is that cus-

tomers need help and advice to select the right items and all the materials they need for a particular job. Customers judge the quality of advice by the appearance of the advisor. An-18-year old school leaver simply lacks the credibility of a worldlywise 55 year old. B & Q set out specifically to attract older staff. Their sales and customer satisfaction levels increased with this change.

You aim to recruit the very best staff available, with the highest level of qualification and the greatest ambition for promotion. Why? If you are creating a flatter organisation with fewer levels of management, you will have fewer opportunities for promotion. Jobs of the future will grow with the individuals ability to expand them. Perhaps high fliers are dangerous. If they consume your valuable training resources and then move on to competitors, maybe they are a hazard to be avoided. Avoid the wonderful people who will not stay. Give consideration to finding the staff with abilities a shade over average, but with a huge loyalty factor.

Where do you find these people?

Often you do not have to find these people – they find you. A recommendation from an existing member of staff must count for something. Two people are putting their reputation on the line for you. Your staff member is making a commitment which says, I believe this person will deliver what the firm needs. Your applicant is promising to live up to that expectation.

In British mining communities the loyalty to the pit has been immense over generations. The whole village knew that its livelihood depended on the success of the mine at the end of the road. All the men in the family expected to work there. It was a calling not a job. Relatives and neighbours worked alongside each other, sharing, supporting and co-operating. These bonding mechanisms served to develop an allegiance that few other organisations could match. Hence, when pits were closed the agony, protest and anger were astonishing to many outsiders. Enormous efforts were made to keep pits open by the families and communities concerned.

An organisation which enthusiastically takes on family members receives a stronger loyalty. A relative of an employee increases the family commitment to the success of your enterprise. You may choose to make a practice of welcoming partners. This is a little like the commitment of single-sourcing supplies. For the couple there needs to be great trust and you must recognise the mutual obligation.

Your reputation as a long-term employer will assist you in attracting applicants which meet your expectations of loyalty.

Thoughts on recruiting

If you are recruiting for a long-term commitment, this will impact on the way you approach the process. For a post at any level, you will want to take a great deal of time and trouble over the selection process. What do eight or ten hours of your time cost, compared with the consequences of the wrong appointment? A person on a wage of $500 per week represents an investment of $1/4 million over ten years. That merits careful assessment.

Look at the track record of candidates in terms of the time lengths they have spent in particular posts, roles and projects. Do they complete tasks? How realistic are their personal ambitions? Can you deliver these expectations?

Interviews are too popular as a method of selection. Even well-trained interviewers following a pattern approach with clearly defined criteria, can make errors when judging the relative merits of different candidates. Reducing the importance of the interview is a sensible approach. There are several ways in which this can be achieved. Enlist the support of the future colleagues. Let them meet the person and explain at length the role, the organisation, the atmosphere and the culture. They will collectively create a truthful picture. Do they feel that the candidate will be assimilated into the team? Does the candidate feel positive about an organisation with vices as well as virtues? If the person you are recruiting will be operating as a telephonist, interview them over the phone to assess their skills in the real role. Even better, recruit from a pool of people known to you and your firm. Use projects, temporary contracts and consultancy assignments to gauge people's skills, effectiveness and cultural fit. Charities frequently use this approach with potential employees. Observing how individuals actually behave is a better form of assessment that making assumptions from dress, bearing and the rehearsed answers to expected questions.

Call up their referees

When you are close to a decision ask for the names of a number of referees. Discuss these referees with the candidate so that you have a view on their depth of experience with the potential recruit. Then make a telephone call to each referee. With a series of prepared open questions find out more about the way the candidate has acted in the past. Take time over this. You are not seeking perfection, but a competent player who will fit within the culture of your organisation. You want someone who will contribute to positive customer relations over the long term.

Don't advertise the post you want to fill

If you recruit for a post below the position you really want, you have some time to assess the person when they are working for you. If your appointment is a success, you can reward the new employee with a promotion. They are motivated by this and you will feel positive about this recognition. If they are not quite as expected, you are dealing with a lesser problem in terms of salaries, seniority and potential disruption.

Resolve mistakes quickly

When you make an error in selection and the new employee is not working out, you owe it to your other staff, the individual concerned and yourself, to resolve it as quickly as possible. Act firmly and swiftly to outplace someone who is not right in terms of skills or attitudes. This should be done with generosity and compassion. It may require help support and guidance as well as appropriate financial compensation. Your generosity has a practical aspect for the unfortunate individual. It also flags up a firm but caring message to existing employees. Finally, it will reflect better on your company in the long term. Word-of-mouth advertising is made up from myriads of little impressions from many sources. Negatives spread faster than positives. Acting positively in every case will not preserve a perfect image, but it will neutralise the potential for a negative image.

Keeping staff

Managing for staff retention gives an added task to the range of management priorities. No single factor retains good staff. Success comes from a cocktail of policies, practices and patterns of behaviour. Your example will pervade through the organisation to deliver a strategy which keeps people loyal and enables you to reap the benefits of lower operational costs and higher quality of service to customers. Each business is different. They have their own characteristics, assets and behavioural liabilities. This checklist may reassure you or may refresh your thinking in how you keep employees. In summary there are five headings:

- Induction.

- Conditions.

- Retention tools.

- Motivation.

- Allegiance.

Induction

You only get one chance to make a first impression. Unlearning an old practice is seven times harder than learning a new practice. Think through extremely carefully the first hour, day and week of a new employee. Will you ever convince them that punctuality is an absolute requirement of your business, if their 9.30 a.m. welcome appointment with you begins fourteen minutes late? Who they meet, and in what sequence, sends subliminal messages about your organisational priorities. Three hours with the financial controller and thirty minutes with customer service is a strong indicator of relative importance. A perception is set up. The memory records what is done more than what is said.

An ideal induction programme has formal elements and informal parts. It consists of meeting key players, observing processes, understanding the business from supply of raw materials all the way to customers (often wholesalers) and end consumers. In the induction at Domino Pizza Stores in Maryland, every newcomer learns that a regular customer is worth $5,000 over the life of a ten-year franchise contract. The best induction has a considered and structured opening, parcels of relevant experience and a final review. This review is not, in reality an end, it is a new beginning. At this review point, the employee is invited to take a personal responsibility for their continued learning. The message is that we have started you off in the firm, but now we shall jointly ensure that you keep growing and learning.

A mentor can play a major part in a successful induction.

High Beeches School in Harpenden, Hertfordshire takes children from age 5 to 11. Each year, every new 5-year old child is given an 11-year-old mentor to guide them through their first school year. It is an astonishingly successful system. It gives confidence, reassurance and a dose of reality to the new child. It reminds the older child of what it is like to see the school afresh, and gives an experience of responsibility. Older children are sharing the induction responsibility with the class teacher of the reception class.

One of the objectives of the induction must be to inculcate an intuitive understanding of how the whole business functions. Again words are inadequate for the task. Demonstration is many times more effective. Interfunctional experience gives that demonstration. Actually spending time in all the different departments, preferably assisting in some practical way with routine and normal tasks gives a true impression of the interdependence of the whole operation. It builds internal relationships and mutual respect. It is harder to let down a member of another department if you know and have worked alongside them.

As an additional benefit, the more linkages there are with a new employee, then the tighter the bonding. If after a month they have met forty people, they will feel a greater sense of belonging than if they had only met a dozen.

A critical need in every induction is time with customers. Jan Carlson said, 'if you are not serving the customer, you had better be helping someone who is.' Everyone in an organisation is part of the product or service delivered to the customer. Hence all need to see where that product or service goes, how it is used. Even a wholly internal staff member can visualise their part in the process.

There were two bricklayers, walking from the pile of bricks to the building site. When asked what they were doing, the first replied, 'I am carrying bricks.' The second gave a different response. 'I am building a cathedral,' he said with pride.

Everyone should feel that they are building a cathedral. Their task must fit clearly in their mind's eye, within the whole scheme of things. When they visit a customer, they can see the end product of their position.

These key parts of an introduction – mentoring, inter-functional experience, time with customers – are necessary for continuing success. The role of the mentor can continue indefinitely. Departments and customers change, so refreshing experiences are needed to keep staff up to date. In point of fact the learning process started with the induction stops only at retirement.

Conditions

There are two aspects to the conditions of work which relate to retention of staff. The first is the reality, the second is the perception. It is standard comment that people spend a long time at work and therefore need to feel comfortable. This means they expect lighting, heating, facilities, cleanliness and convenience. Beyond this are the perceptions. These appear to have a greater impact. For example, a perception that they are the last department on the list for redecoration can be more damaging than the fact that the window frames need a touch of paint. The perception that it is possible for staff to influence their surroundings is more important than any changes that are actually made. The reality and perception of wages and salaries are similar. Expectations need to be carefully managed so that actual outcomes do not disappoint. Key points are managing perceptions of relativity and individual influence.

What really makes people stay?

There are three factors which have a far greater influence on people than their working conditions. Enjoyment of the job, fellowship with colleagues and a feeling of being appreciated are the most powerful tools for retaining staff. Focusing on these three will pay dividends. If these three go awry then dissatisfaction will be expressed in ways which blame other factors. Salaries, working conditions, promotion limits and lack of information will all be highlighted as problems. Concentrate on these central elements of satisfaction. Only inside your organisation can you set out how you will achieve these difficult, but vital aims. There are no textbook answers.

Retention tools

Far behind these three factors in importance are some useful techniques. They have some impact in retention, directly and indirectly, through the message that they convey. Profit sharing is an obvious way of demonstrating the link between good performance with long-term customers and personal reward. There are ways of using profit share to enhance loyalty. On an emotional level, asking employees to vote on how the profit share should be allocated is one way of showing that they can influence how things are recognised. A vote could result in allocation according to team performance, according to ratios of salary or seniority, or on a per capita basis. In any event, staff will own the decision.

On a practical level a profit share can be paid out in instalments. In one scheme, the sum earned was split into thirds. The first portion was paid immediately, the second and third sums after one year and two years respectively. Subsequent payments were not be made if people had left the organisation. Thus long-term loyalty was rewarded with a long term incentive. Incentive payments can also be linked to particular customer accounts, such that if one account is lost a proportion of the profit share is lost. The messages conveyed are that long term employees will benefit from long-term accounts.

Other tools for retention are closely linked to reinforcing fellowship with colleagues and showing appreciation. Length of service awards with recognition ceremonies and newspaper publicity go a long way to illustrating the things that your organisation truly values. You can express it in unique and creative ways. One chain of restaurants pays people a higher wage when they hit 25,000 meals served. A delivery company in Austria recognises the million kilometres stage with a vehicle badge. Salesmen in a brewery can aim for sales volume equivalent to a pile of cases the height of the Empire State Building. The opportunities are legion to create traditions which signal that you value loyalty.

Motivation

We are all different when it comes to motivation. There are certain core assumptions you can make about motivation. Being used to one's full potential is important. Boredom is insidious because it allows time for negative attitudes to develop, and establishes a principle that the job does not need the full efforts of staff to achieve excellent results. Challenge is a valuable input to job satisfaction. Staff, who surprise themselves by reaching previously unachieved levels of performance, swell with pride. Encouraging staff to set themselves performance challenges can pay dividends. Job rotation can break monotony and add interest. The company 3M trains all warehousemen to operate a fork lift truck so that job rotation is possible across all warehouse tasks.

Signs of appreciation have already been mentioned as critical for retention. They are powerful symbols for motivation. In his book, *Making it Happen*, Sir John Harvey-Jones, then Chairman of ICI, wrote:

> I make a habit of sending a certain number of cases of wine each year to individuals at any level in the company who have done something which I have come across which seems to be particuarly meritorious. I send it to the individual's home and I include a personal note from me, thanking him for his achievement.

Rank Xerox give ten president's awards each year with a publicity fanfare across the organisation. The pleasure is in the recognition and the celebration.

Belonging to an organisation or a team is also motivating. Many staff reflect this with a group photograph on the wall have a special name for their department. For example there was the 'ELEPHANT' Department. This was a tongue-in-cheek acronym for 'Endless Labour, Every Possible Hardship And No Thanks!' Fostering and encouraging cameraderie is an important contribution that management can make. From these symbols, standards of team performance can derive. If you have personalised your group of workers with a special name, a badge or 'uniform' and your photograph is on display, perhaps you are all committed to ensuring that your team 'wins'.

This is a creative way to be accepted within a team!

Outsiders will be accepted into this team only if they accept the symbols and standards. A creative example of this is described in Peter de la Billiere's book of the Gulf War, *Storm Command*. His troops are collaborating closely with the American forces. A British officer, Lieutenant Colonel Tim Sulivan, was assigned to work with the American military planners. The Americans were pathologically secretive about their plans and routinely marked them with the classification 'Noforn' – meaning not to be shown to foreigners. Sulivan made himself readily acceptable partly through his easy laid-back manner and partly by the brilliant expedient of donning an American uniform.

Encouraging mental and physical fitness is another way in which management can support motivation. Fit people feel better about everything. Where are your cycle racks and showers for employees who ride to work? Charity connections can also increase motivation through the sense of doing something worthwhile. In both these instances the role of the employer is as enabler. It is providing the opportunity to act in positive and beneficial ways.

An enabling employer might assist staff to set up their own crèche arrangement, with premises, heat and light, but leave staff to organise the system of operation by themselves. In this way the responsibility is clear and the benefit genuinely appreciated.

Allegiance

The final concept for increasing motivation and at the same time encouraging retention of staff is being there in a crisis. By this I mean doing far more than would be expected of an employer

when disaster strikes. For example, when a new employee totally wrecks her car and has no other way of travelling to work, the
manager lends her a company vehicle for a couple of weeks until
she can sort matters out. When there is a death in the family, a
supposedly indispensable player is given unlimited time off at
home with the message, 'Come back when you feel ready'. Giving and not counting the cost in time or money creates an
unbreakable bond. A rival cannot offer a salary to counter the
effect of being there when it was truly needed. The parental emotion of 'How can I help?' sincerely made by a company builds
deep allegiance.

Another human emotion expressed by a corporation can have
a similar effect. It is forgiveness. The terror of having made a
huge mistake on the company's behalf is black and the stuff of
nightmares. Open forgiveness can feel like dramatic liberation to
an employee.

*A new sales manager in a company manufacturing beds made a
fundamental mistake over an order with a major customer, which
resulted in the company losing £10,000 on the transaction. The
customer was important and the relationship was not affected by
this episode. The sales manager believed his career was at an
end when he was called in to the managing director's office.
When the moment came, he said, 'I imagine this is where I hand
you my car keys and leave the company'. To his surprise, the
managing director replied, 'Certainly not. I have just spent
£10,000 training you – I know that you will never make that mistake again! I am looking for a return on that training investment.'
He certainly got it. That sales manager was the top performer in
both of the next two years.*

Forgiveness is not always appropriate, as repeated errors are unaffordable. At the right point they can have a huge impact on an individual and build for you that unassailable allegiance.

An extra point

There is a final point on the subject of recruitment and retention of staff and their complete motivation. Look wider than just employees. Your organisation has a network of suppliers and servicing companies. Some may be large, others one man bands. Select them with care. Meet them with a group of staff before you start doing business. Take references and then build relationships with them. Retain them, for in the same way as changing staff costs money and time, so does changing suppliers. Motivate them as your own staff and you will have a powerful business advantage.

SUMMARY

- Achieving better staff loyalty and retaining experienced staff pays handsomely. A major bank carried out an analysis of the profitability of every branch in its network. The results were overlaid with the length of tenure of the branch manager. The correlation was irresistable. The results showed clearly that branch profitability improved consistently from a low point in a manager's first year to a better position in each of the following four years.

Year 1	1.2%
Year 2	2.5%
Year 3	3.4%
Year 4	3.7%
Year 5	4.3%

- The longer the manager was in post, the more profitable was the branch. Whilst there are more factors at play than simply the manager's length of service, the research does indicate strongly that changing managers too frequently is counter productive.

- Relationship Marketing requires a firm basis of loyal, effective and motivated staff. Before you can build strong and durable relationships with customers, it is essential that you have strong and durable relationships with your staff.

6

SEGMENT SELECTION BY LOYALTY

Customer loyalty is the objective of the organisation seeking success through Relationship Marketing. This chapter looks at the basic building blocks to bring about the best conditions for creating that loyalty. Loyalty is taken as the critical variable. Rather than seeing loyalty simply as a pleasing by-product of an effective marketing strategy, it is taken as an initial objective. From the outset, loyalty building is the core of the marketing strategy. It is not an end, it is the beginning.

Finite markets, mature markets, tough markets

In many Western markets, growth in volume is modest. Low inflation and recession are making growth in value terms difficult to achieve. Whilst there are exceptions, often at the premium sectors and discount basement sectors, most managing directors are looking at finite markets. Worldwide, many products introduced in the past forty years are now selling into mature markets. With this market maturity, margins are threatened. With recession and post recession caution, volumes are restrained. Yet shareholders continue to expect capital appreciation and growing dividends. Without good performance, share prices fall, and vulnerability increases.

Three ways to improve profitability

Convention has it that there are only three ways to increase profitability for an organisation:

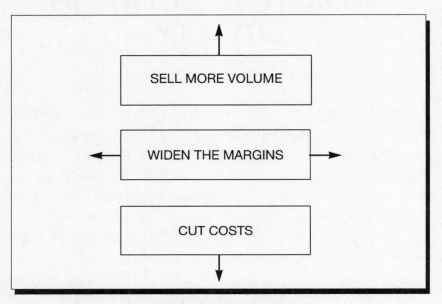

Fig 6.1   Increasing profitability – three methods

Thus, where markets are not growing, and margins are under pressure we have seen enormous pressure on operational costs: supplier margins are squeezed, energy efficiency is increased, business processes are re-engineered, staff are shed, distribution methods are refined. Nevertheless this is a route with limitations. It is about 'how' you carry out your business. Efficiency is always among the objectives of an organisation. It is not however the prime objective. Efficiency gains contribute to profit, they do not generate profit.

As Wayne Jackman, Chief Executive Officer of Pepsico, put it, 'You cannot save your way to prosperity. That alone will not get you there.'

If cutting costs is a small part of the answer, what is the big part?

How can volume be gained in a static or shrinking market? How can margins be widened or even maintained in the business scenarios of the late 1990s?

The answer of course is increased customer loyalty. Greater retention of customers is in many markets or sectors, the only way to improve performance. As we have seen, long term satisfied customers buy more and pay higher margins. Loyalty is the magic substitute for market growth.

So how do you bell the cat?

There is a European children's story. It features a group of mice terrorised by a cat which silently crept up on mice and pounced. At an emergency meeting one mouse proposed a solution – tie a bell to the tail of the cat! Logical, elegant, but very difficult to achieve.

Likewise, the answer to market pressures is enhanced loyalty. It is logical, elegant, but very hard to achieve.

Let us imagine, that you are implementing Relationship Marketing. You have decided that you want to avoid churning your customers. You have convinced your fellow directors. You have selected staff who are likely to be loyal and you motivate them professionally and effectively. What is the next stage?

Obviously you intend to take every step to keep customers once you have attracted them. But there is something you can do beforehand?

Imagine you own a retail store. Two new customers come in and make the same purchase of a Mars Bar. You sell the chocolate bar to both at the same price. Both bars cost you the same. The sales took the same length of time. Which customer is the more valuable? You need more details. During the time you were serving each customer you chatted and found out a little more about them. One is a young New Zealander making a once in a lifetime world trip to London. For some reasons, she has stopped en route *in your shop. The other is 40 to 50 years old, and lives 2 miles away and travels past your shop every day on his way to work. Who might you see again?*

Naturally in business you will give every customer good service, politeness, speed, efficiency. Beyond this, you seek clues to the potential the new customer has to become a loyal and long term. Relationship Marketing is the recognition that some new customers represent better potential for future business and the investment in the relationship with them.

Are all customers the same?

The key issue is the question, are all customers the same as far as loyalty is concerned?

The conclusion is that they are far from the same. For example, according to the Automobile Association, one of the UK's leading private vehicle insurers, 60 per cent of motorists have switched the company providing their car insurance in the past five years. Furthermore, 15 per cent of motorists have changed three or more times. With no further analysis we can see three distinct groups:

Loyal for at least 5 years	40%
Switchers (two or three companies)	45%
Totally disloyal	15%

Which group would you aim to recruit for your future business?

Where would you invest your time, trouble and resources?

Decision made – clearly you want to focus on locating and attracting the customers who exhibit the greatest propensity to stay loyal to a source of supply. Whilst it is possible that you might win a 'totally disloyal' customer and convert them to become loyal to you, the disproportionate costs and effort militate against it.

We want the loyalists! Who are they?

There are some clear steps in identifying which customers you should attract.

Firstly, you analyse the data on your existing customers to determine those who remain most loyal to you. Most consumer brands have a 'core buying club'. Typically for them, your brand would account for 70 per cent of their purchases in that category. Probably these customers represent only 10 per cent of your total customer base. The exercise is to identify these customers and to consider their characteristics.

Secondly, you look carefully at defections. Elementary software can graph the most frequent point of defection. For membership organisations, it is often at the end of year two. Newcomers join, the majority renew after the first year, a big percentage fall off at the second renewal. Those that renew for year three are likely to remain for many years subsequently. Different industries and markets exhibit different patterns. For charities, new donors who are still giving three years later are often lifelong supporters. In fast moving consumer goods markets, the time scale is dramatically shorter, in industrial machinery the time threshold may be very extended.

Who are these defectors? What is distinctive about them? To establish meaningful data, it may be necessary to categorise the defectors, by ostensible reason for defection. They will not all be leaving for the same reason. People who experienced a service shortfall and departed may differ from those who received exemplary standards, yet still defected. One useful analysis is to consider from their point of view, whether you were their most suitable supplier. If you could not be, then the loss had an inevitability about it. The analysis will then show:

- Lost customers for whom we were not the most suitable supplier

- Lost customers who experienced errors/poor service

- Lost customers – not readily explicable

All three groups require study, subdivision, and analysis to arrive at an understanding of the dynamics of desertion. You need a very clear picture of who defects and why?

Thirdly, you compare the two groups across every possible dimension. In which ways do the loyalists differ from those who defect? A major bank had dramatically different patterns of customer defection. The analysis revealed the discriminating difference was age at which full time education ceased. New customers joining the bank who left school at 16 years of age tended to remain life long loyal. Typically they needed 3 significant account problems within 24 months before they moved banks. New customers with graduate level qualifications had a lower propensity to remain with the bank and a significantly lower tolerance of errors and misunderstandings. A second dimension which often shadowed the first dimension was level of earnings. The more a person earned, the lower was the probability of a long term banking relationship.

Segment by loyalty

The Relationship Marketing approach to delivering long term loyalty is to segment your markets using degrees of loyalty as the discriminating factor. You may segment using loyalty as an absolute dimension, or it is possible to use other segmentation dimensions as proxies for loyalty.

Segmentation is the division of a total market into meaningful groups, each with discernably different requirements. You then select the group or groups which are attractive to you, and whose different needs you are able to meet with superior value. This is the essence of marketing. The essence of Relationship Marketing is to select those groups who demonstrate a higher propensity to be loyal to their supply source, product or brand.

In consumer markets, classically, there are four basic segmentation typologies: geographic, demographic, psychographic and behavioural. In effect these will be managed in combinations to achieve best results.

Segmentation typologies

- **Geographic** – nation, region, city size, urban/suburban/rural, climate.

- **Demographic** – age, sex, family size, family stage, income, occupation, education.

- **Psychographic** – social class, personality, lifestyle.

- **Behaviour** – rate of use, occasions of use, attitude to the product, loyalty, benefits sought, product experience.

Lavish attention has been paid to geo-demographic systems of segmentation since the late 1970s. With escalating sophistication and reducing cost, census data is carefully matched with household neighbourhood types. Direct marketers have sophisticated sorting and sifting approaches to utilise the full power of software capabilities and the information available.

In the 1980s advertising agencies and marketing managements invested considerable attention on personality and lifestyle based segmentation systems to replace the diminishing usefulness of the class-based systems previously utilised.

The typology which has received least attention by practitioners has been behaviour. Yet how people have behaved would appear to be one of the best predictors of how they will behave in the future. Also, the way one group behaves can be so significantly different from the actions of another group, that they merit completely separate attention.

Behavioural segmentation

Segmenting customers and potential customers by their behaviour embraces a number of approaches, some of which are listed above. For Relationship Marketing the two most valuable approaches are Usage and Loyalty.

In recent marketing, Pizza Hut have focused on two segments. In contrast with mass marketing directed at a wide variety of actual and potential customers Pizza Hut has categorised its customers, by their frequency and scale of patronage, and is targeting the groups defined as heavy and medium users of its delivery service. Employing incentives, competitions and data-base marketing techniques they have captured information on customers which enables them to mail appropriate and different messages to build sales with both groups. For example: heavy users are given vouchers which must be redeemed within four weeks and are encouraged to buy special value meals deals. On the other hand medium users have a longer period of voucher currency – eight weeks – commensurate with their different purchasing patterns. Both groups also receive a questionnaire with an incentive for its completion and return on the next visit. This provides further information on usage and how it may be increased.

Usage can be contrasted with non-usage and appropriate messages provided. Understanding why non-users are not taking advantage of a product or service can assist converting them to usage and also indicating ways in which you can enhance the relationship with users.

British Telecom offered a charge card and a large number of people elected to receive this card. However they discovered that in effect there was a 'dead zone' of people who had applied for cards, but had not used them for twelve months. Back in the marketplace of 200 years ago, if someone asked for a service and then never took it up the simple question would have been asked. That is exactly what British Telecom did. They wrote to each of these signed-up non-users. On the outside of the envelope was printed an image of the charge card, as a reminder. Inside was a reply paid card with three big tick option boxes: OK, Help, Cancel. In other words are you happy with your card, do you require help or guidance in its use, or is it simply to be cancelled? By speaking to customers so directly and straightforwardly, they earned a response from 52 per cent of the non-users.

Immediately the outlay was covered by the saved cost of issuing new cards to those who did not want them. For the remainder, usage was stimulated and much was learnt about the support and education of new users which is being built into future customer recruitment. This occurs in two ways. Firstly it indicated which types of customer represented the best potential. Secondly it helped to determine how best to attract and guide them.

Product experience is another aspect of behavioural segmentation. Segmentation could be by the customer's familiarity with the product or service. This could range from 'experienced long-time user' to 'customer of two to four years' standing' to 'first-time buyer'. Mortgage lenders frequently categorise house buyers in this way. As we have already seen, loyal and long-established customers require less help and guidance, than product virgins. The need for a careful and planned induction for customers will be covered later.

Segmenting by loyalty

As a direct attribute, loyalty can be used as one of the behavioural dimensions. You may classify people by degrees of loyalty. This chart demonstrates the range of loyalty patterns. The three symbols (* # +) represent three different competing products.

Segment	Pattern	Description
Unquestioned loyalty	########	Will always purchase from you
Normal choice	###*##*#	Routinely purchase from you, but also buy competing products
Could be swayed	***#####	Loyal at heart, but not necessarily to you
Promiscuous	*+#*+#+*	No loyalty shown. May be variety driven or price obsessed

Classifying customers by the loyalty patterns they display provides a route to the appropriate treatment to move them up the ladder of loyalty, where this is possible. If it is not possible it allows strategies to optimise profitable buying patterns or to shed the customer harmoniously.

Next is a UK retail fashion chain. In 1988 they established a second channel of distribution, a mail order catalogue called Next Directory, *featuring up-market clothing – often before the apparel appeared in the stores. The catalogue attracted 500,000 users in the first season and 300,000 new users in each subsequent season. However, around 90,000 customers dropped out each season. To address this costly failure rate, Next classified customers in five bands:*

'Top Shoppers'	*– 25 per cent of customers accounting or 50 per cent of sales*
'Active'	*– the majority of their customers*
'Dormant'	*– previously active customers with no recent purchases*
'Non-orderers'	*– received catalogue but had never placed an order*
'New'	*– new catalogue requests*

Communication is tailored specifically to each group. The 'Top Shoppers' are the most valuable. They receive their catalogues before other customers, which means that their orders are almost always met from full stock, thereby reducing the risk of disappointment from out of stock items. They also receive regular informative and promotional mailings. 'New' customers also receive the same service until their pattern of purchases is established. 'Active' customers receive their catalogues next, ahead of

the 'dormants', and they will also see selected mailings. Cus-
tomers are not made aware of these differences in treatment
since they may be moved between categories. As a result of this
exercise, the dropout rate has fallen to 2 per cent per season.
More than half their customers have been buying for two years or
longer. Bad debt has diminished accordingly.

(Source: *Marketing Week Customer Loyalty Supplement*, 15 October 1993).

This illustrates a method of segmenting by loyalty pattern and demonstrates the benefits accrued from such approaches in a consumer market.

Industrial market segmentation

In industrial markets, the classical approach was outlined by Thomas V. Bonoma and Benson P. Shapiro in *Segmenting the Industrial Market* (Lexington Books, 1983). They highlighted five major variables:

- Demographic – Company location, company size, industry type.

- Operating variables – High/low need for service, heavy/light users, technologies.

- Purchase approaches – Central/decentralised, finance/engineering driven.

- Situational factors – Urgency, order size, special applications.

- Personal characteristics – Attitude to risk, companies with similar values, loyalty.

Surprisingly little has been written on segmentation in business-to-business markets. Even so, the concept of the fifth variable has been neglected. This implies the deliberate categorisation of actual and potential customers into those with whom we might be able to succeed over the long term and those where there is less certainty.

Every company has a personality – do you like the personality of your customers?

Each company has its own corporate culture, style and persona. It is, in essence, 'the way things are done around here'. An analysis of company styles among your customers can yield a number of positive and negative points.

Some companies enjoy risk. They revel in change, variety and novelty. Uncharted territory attracts them? They experiment with people, products, processes and markets. Other companies can be classed as risk averse. They need reassurance, personal attention and support. They aim to minimise risk and danger and play safe with people and markets. Neither is right or wrong. Different industries, markets, cultures demand different styles. Each has its advantages. However, ask yourself, which is the more likely to continue trading with you over the duration? Probably the more risk averse organisation. For long term loyalty, should you seek out risk averse companies?

As a counterpoint to this, look at companies with similar values. If your organisation is thriving, radical, risk taking and experimental, which of the two types of company above will feel most comfortable? Probably the company which thrives on variety, change and experiment itself. Matching your values and the values of your customers is enormously powerful in terms of creating common understanding. When there is common ground, familiar outlooks and joint attitudes, decisions are easier, negotiations faster and harmony greater.

This is not a panacea. It is a selective technique. Where you are able to find like companies with which to trade it is extremely

synergistic. Perhaps only 10 per cent of your customers will fall
into this typology. Using Relationship Marketing approaches, it
is possible to work successfully with most organisations.

The third point related to loyalty. Some customers are inherently more loyal than others. They display it in their behaviour.
When asked, they will reveal the number of suppliers used over a
period. You can use this to select out the customers who are
unlikely to remain with you.

*An American health insurance company found that some client
companies were buying purely on price. Service levels were not
important to them. Simply they sought the cheapest quotation.
This resulted in switching every year. The cost and disruption
was seen as unaffordable. The strategy put volume ahead of
profit and efficient operations. Thus they instructed their brokers
not to write any policies for companies who had switched suppliers more than twice in the previous five years. Results were
dramatic. They were able to provide better service to the clients
who appreciated service factors, and operate more effectively.
Profit and loyalty increased in step.*

Of course, you never need to say no. Like the artisan builder
who does not wish to carry out a particular job, you simply quote
a price which will cover your costs in a very short-term relationship. If they buy, so be it. You then must ensure that you do not
over-service these clients at the expense of your loyal custom.

'Segmenting customers in mature industrial markets' is the
title of an article by Rangan, Moriarty and Swartz in the *Journal
of Marketing*, October 1992. Based on an analysis of twelve variables, they have constructed a model with four segments:

Segment	Description	Motivation
Programmed buyers	small customers/ less price sensitive	purchase is a routine
Relationship buyers	small customers/more knowledgeable	seek partnership
Transaction buyers	large customers/very knowledgeable	balance price/ service
Bargain hunters	large customers/ willing to switch readily	price/service sensitive

Using this model, Rangan, Moriarty and Swartz recommend separate strategies for each segment. For the programmed buyers, they propose that sales people focus on managing the decision-making processes and understanding the ways to influence them. For the bargain hunters, the strategy would be to focus on adding service rather than cutting prices, but with tact and care since these customers are likely to account for a large proportion of sales. For relationship buyers, personal contact is critical and needs to be built into their account management structure. For transaction buyers the approach is to meet their service needs in a way which will inhibit their migration towards the bargain hunter segment.

Interestingly, this article suggests with a theoretical basis, that the correct approach is to assess what the different customer types are really seeking out of a long-term relationship. Then you aim to provide it, in a profitable context.

Customer acquisition

Segmenting your total market into actual and potential customers with varying degrees of inherent loyalty is the core of the Relationship Marketing strategy. The execution is about identifying the customers who tend to be most loyal, and seeking to acquire more customers with similar characteristics. Specifically, you should aim to avoid attracting customers who will consume your marketing, financial and human resources, and then switch suppliers before you can receive any payback.

Your own company analysis offers the best guide to the nature, location and attributes of the loyal customers, to enable you to prospect for more like them. There are some starting points which may suggest useful directions for this analysis.

What sort of prospects might make loyal customers?

There are twelve directional pointers to potential loyalists. These are based on practical experience from a variety of industries. Therefore they may or may not apply particularly to your business.

1 **Referrals are better prospects than people who respond to advertisements.** This applies to industrial and consumer markets. Someone who comes to you because of the recommendation of a friend, family member or business colleague, will be more likely to stay with you than the respondent to a mailing or advertisement. There are several reasons for this. Firstly, there is the screening process that has taken place in the recommender's mind. He has matched you with the consumer, using his knowledge. Secondly, we have a personal bond, a link with a known quantity. Loyalty to you becomes an extension of the loyalty to the friend or colleague. Finally, there is the strength of the recommendation itself. This means that if the initial experience is not totally satisfactory, there is a tendency to forgive and persist, derived from the thought that an expert put you here and there must have been a reason. Everything you can do to foster referrals

will build the loyalty pattern of your customer base.

2 **Long courtships are better than short ones.** Like human relationships, whirlwind romances can turn out to be one night stands. Those customers who take a long time to woo, and who insist on getting to know you well, before you do business, are most likely to stay with you for the duration. It is always worthwhile targeting attractive potential customers who are happy with their existing supplier and investing time in understanding them and building up a rapport. The customers who are hardest to prise away from competitors will be the hardest to prise away from you when you have won them. Long-term relationship building is the answer.

3 **People who buy at the standard price are better than promotion respondents.** The customers who have been enticed in by your price offers always carry that price influence. They will have an intuitive feeling that your original prices were at the correct level. Moving to standard prices subsequently will create a subconscious dissonance. They may not express it, but it is a perpetual threat to business continuity. Price promotions also attract the price obsessed buyers. They will push for better prices or leave. This can consume your time and discount budget. The challenge is to attract customers who will appreciate the standard price structure – more difficult, but more beneficial in the long run.

4 **The risk averse are better than the experimenters.** As we have stated above, the experimentalist customers will be enthusiastic to come to you as a new and different supplier, but they will be equally enthusiastic to move on to a new supplier. Seek the cautious buyers.

5 **Small-scale purchasers may be more loyal than the**

mega-buyers. This is not always true, but it may be a hypothesis worth testing in your customer base. Unless your business depends for its cost structure on a very large volume, you may find that the relatively smaller customers provide greater stability.

6 **Local customers can be better than long distant buyers.** There are a number of reasons why this may be true. Partly more local is also more familiar. The influence direct and indirect is greater the more local you are. There is a higher incidence of recommendation and informal contact. There may also be a pre-disposition to buy from a firm nearer rather than further, for security or comfort or regional loyalty. Nationally the concept works better in some countries than others. It is a potential angle to adopt for your customer analysis. Make the most of the local connection where it exists.

7 **Customers looking for high levels of service.** Some customers are less service literate than others. By 'service literate', I mean that good service is sought, recognised and appreciated. Some customers appear unaware of the benefits of high levels of service. They will not refuse them, but neither will they appreciate them sufficiently to pay a premium. A key part of Relationship Marketing is the way the understanding is built through service provision. Therefore as a guide to customer selection, it may be helpful to screen out those customers who are less service literate.

8 **Customers with special needs.** Certain groups of customers may exhibit a requirement for extra service. For example in the manufacture of explosive substances, extreme care is essential as far as fire risk is concerned. Suppliers must be highly sensitive about this. In consumer markets, older customers, for instance, may have specific needs for their com-

fort. Holiday resorts may reflect this with the provision of easier access, well lit stairways, better provision of toilets and rest rooms. Lands' End – the mail order clothing company – offer wider fittings to accommodate the physique of older buyers. In all these cases, industrial and consumer, discretion is an important factor. None of these customers wish these special needs to be broadcast. If you can find groups of customers who have special needs, and meet them, their loyalty co-efficient will be substantially higher.

9 **Customers seeking a high level of personalisation.** These customers are looking for someone who will recognise their individuality. Their expectations of support are greater than the average customer. This may be a real need, or simply a perception in the mind of the buyer. In either event, meeting a request for personalisation can create the loyalty bond these customers are seeking. For example: Ladbrokes – the UK's largest betting shop chain – launched 'Manager's Special Offers'. Managers were able to select 24 special offers from a centrally produced menu of 50. These included improved odds, discounted stakes, and free bets for bulk purchase. By giving the manager a way of personalising the bet, the gamblers were able to feel they were receiving something special, local, individual and personal from the manager. The result is that customer loyalty among these groups is enhanced.

10 **Customers at a critical phase in their lives/businesses.** When a business expands from its original premises to a larger facility, or opens its first branch outlet, or floats on the stock exchange, the management feel very aware of the transition. Critical phases are an opportunity moment for loyalty seekers. If you can be there and actively support the company at this juncture, then you have a strong likelihood of being

treated as an 'insider' and a favoured supplier for the long term. Similarly, in consumer markets, people pass through vulnerable phases. Tampon manufacturers well understand this and expend prodigious efforts to provide sympathetic advice and guidance at the onset of menstruation, so that women will remain loyal thereafter. Marriage is another critical phase where retailers and service industry providers can benefit in the long run, by extending understanding service. See how the department store leads couples through the selection process for wedding gift dinner services and crockery, as an example of how to handle consumers at critical phases.

11 **Demographic groups can give signals towards loyalty.** Frequently in consumer markets, home owners will behave more loyally than renters, the middle-aged and elderly will exhibit greater loyalty than the young, the rural customers will be less fickle than their urban counterparts. In industrial markets, family firms will often be more loyal than multinationals, high status brand owners more loyal than commodity suppliers, engineering-dominated concerns less prone to supplier switching than financially driven outfits.

12 **High mobility is a danger sign.** Customer categories who move frequently are the most difficult to make loyal. For example, military personnel are liable to be relocated large distances, at short notice. Their attitudes are shaped by an awareness of this. Building relationships with their suppliers is not part of this attitude. Students, musicians and entertainers can fall in the same category. It is not impossible to achieve loyalty from highly mobile groups, and examples exist. However, it is a specialist area and needs particular focus on these individuals to succeed.

These points are all clues to set you analysing your customer base for the best predictors of loyalty, so that you can orientate your recruitment towards the customer types who are more likely to remain with you.

A word of caution

To give a word of warning, there is a danger that pursuing narrowly a strategy of selecting only the most loyal customers leads to a niche approach. Each of the above suggestions could result in a customer acquisition procedure so refined that you are constrained into running a small-scale operation. This is not necessary. The key concept is that on a scale of loyalty, there is a continuum of customers. At one end of the scale are people whose loyalty once won will never be shaken. At the other end of the scale is the butterfly who will never sip nectar at the same flower twice. Your management skill and judgement determines where on this scale you wish to draw the line. In effect you are balancing volume opportunity with customer loyalty. The wider your selection of customers, the less loyal will be the average customer. Wherever you mark the scale with a cut-off point, you will be better off than the competitor who does not operate a true strategy of customer acquisition by potential loyalty.

The myth of customer loyalty schemes

In the early 1990s a plethora of loyalty schemes were promulgated. American 'frequent flyer programmes' flourished to the extent that points were included in more than one divorce settlement. They were embraced by European and Far Eastern airlines. American Express 'membership miles' were extended to the French market in 1993, linking loyalty points schemes for their charge card with those run by airlines like Swissair, Air France, SAS and Austrian Airlines. Oil companies dreamt up card collection devices, where stickers were given out by the gallonage or litres bought, to be redeemed for gifts. Sophisticated concepts included cards with magnetic stripes which could accumulate your points and be used as currency in a particular retail chain.

Microsoft customers in the United States, Britain, France and Germany, fill in registration cards after purchasing Microsoft products which are swapped for points depending on the amount purchased. When enough points have been collected, consumers can exchange them for the company's software products.

If personal possessions are not the motivator, then astute retailers allow you to collect their vouchers on behalf of schools so they may be redeemed for textbooks or computers.

Can loyalty be bought . . .?

These loyalty programmes are often a substitute for genuine loyalty building in the Relationship Marketing concept. By contrast Air Miles is a brand in its own right, built on the platform of British Airways service excellence. You *earn loyalty, you cannot buy it.*

The myth of loyalty through price promotion

Price promotions are always cited by consumers as the most attractive. Typically when you research customers with a list of attributes which will lead them to buy a product or service, around 80 per cent will flag price reduction, discount or extra value as the first item. If you responded literally to the research then you would forever be offering special price promotions. It is true that these promotions attract new customers. Adopting this strategy will give you a revolving set of new customers. Price promotion does not create loyalty.

There are four dangers of a price promotion strategy:

- **Price promotions attract more defectors than loyalists.**
  The new custom brought in by a price promotion will be
  least inclined to stay with you, when your prices no longer
  appear the best value. They have not selected you for the
  durable virtues of trust, understanding, compatibility, flexibility, adaptability, reliability, expertise, knowledge, technological leadership and so on. They have chosen you for
  cheapness, which is often a transient virtue.

- **Price promotions teach customers to buy on price.**
  Advertising has an informative and educational aspect,
  teaching your customers about the product and its features,
  uses, strengths, advantages and benefits. Communication
  which stresses price as the major reason for purchase will
  influence and convince future customers, younger buyers and
  new users that price is the important dimension. A price promotion today is an investment in customer training that will
  give you lower returns in the future.

- **Price promotions often distort the volume and time relationship.** Price promotions can bring orders forward. A history of price promotions by season as in the soft-drink
  industry results in customers holding orders for the next
  price promotion. Hence you achieve a double bunching
  effect. This radically increases cost and efficiency of production and distribution. You build into the cycle costly volume
  surges and drops. Forecasting becomes increasingly difficult
  on a pattern of artificially distorted figures.

- **Price promotions can annoy existing customers.** When a
  loyal and happy customer sees that the price with which he is
  satisfied is actually a premium price, he is frustrated. When a

regular user sees that a one-off buyer is cherry-picking a better price than she receives for her long-term business, she is angry. When a major user discovers that he is subsidising new business, he takes his custom elsewhere.

Price promotion is tantalisingly attractive in the short term, but deceptively expensive in the long term. The most effective pricing strategies are those that are delightfully inconspicuous. Price represents such continuing and reassuring good value that it never attracts attention to itself.

The Mars Bar represents, in most markets, the kind of value for money which no other chocolate manufacturer could replicate. They could not assemble the ingredients for the retail price charged by Mars. Yet Mars do not run price promotions. They stress the quality of the recipe, the excellence of the chocolate, the energy, the richness. The Mars Bar has shadowed the indices of retail prices and offers every day low price. **They never say this.** *To do so would be detrimental to the image. 'Buy us we are cheap' is a poor banner, compared with 'Buy us we are rich, indulgent, and pleasure giving'.*

Across the world, the mid 1990s will probably be heralded as the age when annual inflation ceased to be an automatic component of pricing strategies. The history of downward inflexibility of prices is over. Prices can and will fall in real terms in many markets. Where quantity surveyors in the UK in 1990 were charging 2.5 per cent for overseeing a building contract, they now charge 2 per cent. Computer networking software is reducing in price by 20 per cent per year. Marlboro, Proctor & Gamble and other major consumer goods companies have scrambled to reduce prices. Others are following.

In this price scenario, promotional pricing becomes even more dangerous. The lesson must be to focus on providing increasingly good value on a continuing basis. Begin with your best and most loyal customers, so that price never enters the arena as a debating point. Good prices should be implicit in your behaviour, not stressed as a reason for loyalty.

Real loyalty comes from real differentiation

Real loyalty does not derive from a bonus token or a 5 per cent discount. More important than loyalty cards, incentives and special price promotions is the commitment to a different and better service, which the customer understands. The last phrase is critical, customers must understand that you are different and in what precise way this is better for them. Where your pricing strategy is discreet and implicit, the differentiation strategy should be clear and explicit. The consequences of real differentiation are dramatic. According to the Henley Centre Planning for Social Change, most marketing problems are the perceived weaknesses in the company's offer or the absence of a sense of its unique qualities.

Real differentiation is increasingly hard to sustain. In computers, oil, motor cars, beer, office stationery, accounting services and audio equipment we quietly feel that there is no difference between the products of the major half-dozen suppliers. We do not shout out this sense of homogeneity, but it is a backdrop to our thinking. Why therefore should a consumer be loyal to a supplier? Why should he or she not buy on price?

Two ways to differentiate . . .

The role of the company is to create a difference and convince a set of customers that this difference exists and is relevant to them.

It is worth paying and staying. The difference can come from hard or soft areas. By hard I mean tangible product and perform-ance differences – faster, stronger, more durable, more sensitive . . . Soft differences come through personal contact. The hard dif-ferences are often replicable by rivals. The soft differences are a quantum leap harder to copy. It is personal experience that cre-ates loyalty not competitive activity or the product.

The Rapp & Collins Partnership carried out extensive research to understand why customers were lost. Their findings illustrate the value of personal contact.

Reason	Percentage
Moved away or died	4%
Relationships with other companies	5%
Competitive activity	10%
Product dissatisfaction	14%
No contact, indifference, attitude of sales force	65%

The chilling conclusion is that for many customers the defec-tion was simply a consequence of lack of attention and contact. Most customers need to feel wanted and appreciated. Recognis-ing this from the outset is a critical part of the expectation setting process with new customers.

Training the new customer

Customers form impressions from their first contact, but these become established with the first real experience of your product or service. We looked at how the concentration on price as a dis-criminator taught customers what to value. The initial experience shapes the customers expectations. You should manage this introductory phase as carefully as you would manage the induction of a new employee.

You only get one chance to give a first impression

The first impression of a person, a building, a department or a company is the impression which endures. In *Marketing* magazine, the designer Michael Peters asked why so many reception areas are so badly designed. This is the first point of contact and where first impressions are formed. He wrote:

Imagine . . . you walk into an area that is so over-lit that you feel you are about to be given the third degree. You are confronted by a burly security guard who proffers you a seat on a stained chair in front of a table on which are backdated and torn copies of magazines and newspapers. This immediately gives you a negative impression of the company you are about to meet.

On the other hand . . . you walk into a calm, simple and well lit waiting area. You are greeted by a receptionist who takes your coat and sits you down in modestly designed surroundings with a cup of coffee (in a proper cup and saucer) and the day's newspapers.

Which company would you like to do business with?

With your premises, people, packaging, point of sale consider the impact on a first time observer. What first impression will they create in the mind of that potential new customer?

You only get one chance to set the customer's expectations

Moving on from the first impression, how do you brief a new customer? If your salesman promises a new account a monthly service visit by the technical division, then ten visits in a year is a shortfall and is seen as a service failure. If the promise was of a visit at least quarterly, then the same number of visits would probably be seen as a pleasing over delivery on expectations. The skill is in a marginal degree of under-promising and a commitment to over delivering.

'I can't make your machine work!'

New users are never as familiar with the product or service as you will be. They need an induction programme – though you may not herald it as such. For example, Burger King teach you a special language which includes abnormal vocabulary like 'Regular fries and a Whopper please'. You did not intuitively come up with that form of words, they taught you. Consider the use of your vocabulary and how it can be used consistently. How and where do you explain these terms to new users? Buyers of very fast motor cars are often given high speed tuition on a circuit as a part of the purchase arrangement. Did the vendor of your video recorder take time to teach you the function of each of the controls? Would that have helped?

What happens when the honeymoon is over?

The promises, behaviours, courtesies experienced in the initial trading or buying period are also taken as the benchmark. Any retreat from these will be seen as a problem. This is a critical point. Working with many companies, the over-focus on looking after new customers can be counter-productive. Unsustainable attention is poured over them, then they are succeeded by another new customer and the sense of neglect arises. In the management of new customers the four precepts are:

- Create a positive first impression.

- Set realistic expectations by what you say and (especially) by what you do.

- Train them in product/service use.

- Avoid the sense of disappointment, when the novelty wears off.

A radical suggestion

When you recruit a new employee, you brief them as you do a new customer. When you take on a new employee, frequently you provide them with training and I suggest you do the same with new users. You find mentors for new staff. Why not do the same with new customers. Introduce them to an established customer who will act as counsellor to the new user. This suggestion goes beyond the obvious applications in business to business marketing. It can apply also in the marketing of consumer durables. For example, introducing the new buyer to a user group or owners' club, or simply giving (with permission) the name of a neighbouring established customer.

SUMMARY

- The theme of this chapter has been that your strategy of securing a loyal customer base begins before anything else. You need to seek out those customers who have the greatest propensity to remain loyal to you. They need to be distinguished from the less loyal segments and attracted. Loyalty vouchers and cheap prices are not the best mechanic for attraction – go for products and staff that are different and better. Having attracted them you need to train them and set the appropriate expectations so that they continue to be satisfied customers. Like belling the cat, this is not easy. Here is an example of a company who carry this out to marked effect.

A champion of customer loyalty is State Farm Insurance. Founded 70 years ago, they now insure around 20 per cent of US households. Initially they operated in farming communities, but then moved to cover towns and cities. They have an $18 billion capital base. They have the lowest sales and distribution costs among like companies, yet their agent incomes are higher. They aim to serve better than average drivers.

Their Relationship Marketing approach works as follows. Staff are not moved frequently, but encouraged to become established in their community, so they are able to build long lasting relationships in person. For example, agents will target their customers' teenage offspring. Training customers was mentioned above – they will speak to them about safe driving before they take to the road. Agents lecture at High Schools on the perils of drink driving and careless driving. Young drivers are encouraged to be more careful. Their parents are grateful. The State Farm Insurance agents read the local papers and deliberately give discounts to people who get high grades as a form of recognition.

Unlike many of their competitors who hunt constantly for new business, their agent commission is at the same level for new or renewal. Repeat business is just as valuable as conquest sales.

With Relationship Marketing strategies like these in practice, they achieve a retention rate of over 90 per cent.

7

THE LEARNING ORGANISATION

Arie De Geus, Head of Planning at Royal Dutch Shell, said that the ability to learn faster than your competitors may be the only sustainable competitive advantage. In other words, competitive advantage is a relative concept and it is time based. Hence an organisation's effectiveness in learning is its primary strength. Successful organisations must be learning organisations.

What is learning, and what is a learning organisation?

Learning is the process of gaining knowledge, skill or ability. For the organisation it implies the acquiring knowledge of products, customers, markets and competitors, then understanding its significance and finally determining the opportunity it represents. This is an interactive process of response to change and constant test and experimentation with feedback at every stage. The objective is the application in practical ways of the lessons learnt so as to anticipate the market. Anticipation of needs adds value to the relationship with the customer. The relationship is strengthened. Thereby competitive advantage is maintained or enhanced.

In model format the definition of the learning organisation would appear thus:

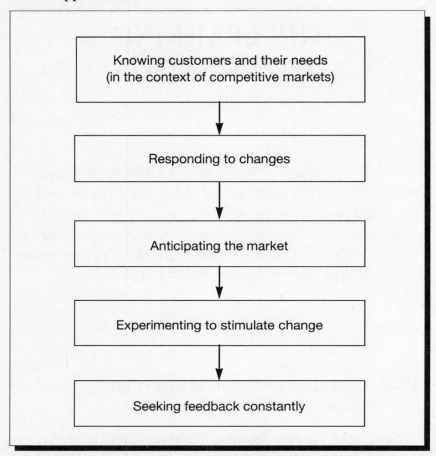

This chapter will follow this sequence in order to explore the ways to be effective as a learning organisation.

Know your customer

Knowing their customers proved a significant cost-saving benefit to Whirlpool Corporation USA in summer 1993. Computer monitoring of a new model washing-machine highlighted a leakage problem. As *Business Week* reported on 21 March 1994:

It seemed that after just a few washloads, the machines were springing bad leaks. As soon as the Whirlpool engineers determined the cause – a faulty hose clamp – manufacturing was immediately halted. More important though, Whirlpool's computer helped identify each of the few hundred customers who had purchased the machines so that mechanics could be sent out to replace the offending part. 'Imagine the property damage liability if there had been a leak in a fifth floor apartment,' reflects Gary Lockwood, Whirlpool's director of consumer assistance.

Rectifying a problem, before the customer knew it existed, is the outcome of relationship marketing for the customer.

For Marriot Hotels, knowing their customers is their lifeblood, as mentioned in Chapter 2.

Through their computer system, the Marriot receptionist knows, as a customer checks in, whether he appreciates an iron in his room, whether she prefers a non-smoking room on the first floor, whether the bill will be customer-settled, sent to the firm, or charged to a monthly account, whether the customer is a member of the Diamond Club and entitled to an upgrade. This information is an important element in Marriot's strategy to stay ahead through customer knowledge.

Respect the knowledge you have of your customer.

Knowledge alone is insufficient. Critical is the sensitive application of this knowledge. Marriot well understand that a loud public announcement across reception that 'The database says you want a non-smoking room near an elevator,' is an abuse of the relationship. Discretion is all. The receptionist will smoothly ask if room 2006 will suit the guest, adding that it is near the lift on the non-smoking floor. The right service simply appears to occur naturally. The customer slips into 'Yes' mode, confirming the suggestions made by the receptionist.

Knowledge includes contact experience

Likewise, British Airways have an Executive Club for frequent fliers, who carry a card.

Swiping the Executive Club card at the check-in reveals favourite seats and dietary requirements. Additionally the database details how often and where they have flown on previous flights. This indicates their awareness of the particular destination. If new, assistance can be offered. If familiar, then this can be acknowledged.

All this reminds the customer that he or she is seen as a unique individual.

For a finance house, contact experience is a vital part of the database. A mailing promoting personal loans might cause real offence to a customer whose loan application has just been turned down. Pre-qualification can be another asset of the database. Offence is also created by a mis-spelt name, title or address. The nightmare mailing for an insurance company is a life assurance offer directed to a deceased customer.

Database requirements

Thus the requirements for your database are that it is accurate and up to date. It must also be accessible and relevant. Accessibility is important in a large and complex organisation, where more than one party may have reason to contact the customer. A promotional arm may need the data as much as the warranty or service section. Geographically separate operations can use and update the same live data-bases through Groupware like Lotus Notes.

Relevance is also critical. There are two conflicting temptations within database design. The first is to add more and more fields of information – who knows when it may assist in a conjoint analysis or a sophisticated segmentation exercise based on unusual common attributes? There is a diminishing cost argument against multi-field databases. With the increasing speed of computing at ever decreasing cost, this is less a barrier. The true drawback is the up-dating, since old data can be worse than no data. The limitations are human not computer based. Can you really abstract and discern shape and meaning from more than ten bits of data? Most executives slip into averaging when too many variables blur the meaning.

Creative use of data

The database is not creative – that is your role. If you really know your customers and how they behave as buyers, then maybe there are windows of opportunity.

US branches of Ratners chain of jewellers routinely captured partners' birth dates, so that they could helpfully suggest a potential gift shortly before the next birthday arose. In the United States, where you can pay agencies to provide this type of reminder, the service was valued.

Volvo owners have great pride in their cars and are renowned for talking 'over the fence' to their neighbours. The whole theory of socio-demographics places like-minded residents together in communities.

In one market, Volvo took the addresses of recent purchasers and mailed houses adjacent and opposite that buyer. A low cost and creative and reportedly successful approach derived from infor-mation they already possessed.

Knowledge is more than a database, it is understanding customers

Of course, knowledge is more than just a database. It is about a collective company understanding of the nature of the customer and his or her buying process. Who are the buyers? Buyers of fast food are frequently the parents of the children who consume the food. Hence McDonalds must understand the psyche of the buyer and the consumer. Thus, the concern of the parents for cleanliness is addressed by the visible evidence of cleaners sweeping floors and wiping tables around you. The desires of the children are encouraged by Ronald McDonald with his colourful promotions. Who are the influencers? In the People's Republic of China, selling Trane air conditioning means persuading the consultants and architects to make that recommendation to the Chinese specifiers. There are other roles. In some buying situations you must pass through a secretary to reach the buyer. DHL – the express parcel courier service – have run environmentally orientated promotions and information campaigns aimed at 'Green'-conscious secretaries, simply to gain access to the buyer. Even the buyer does not necessarily make the decisions. She or he will normally recommend to a superior in a commercial transaction. A partner or parent may finally make the decision in a domestic purchase.

So how do you enter this process labyrinth? How do you map the process and make sense of it? How do you develop an appropriate strategy for employing the understanding in order to build the relationship and hence sales?

Get close to the customer

The conventional (and correct) answer is to get close to the customer. Japanese executives in consumer goods companies like Toshiba will spend significant lengths of time visiting individual customers, asking them to describe in detail how they decided to buy, why Toshiba, what factors were involved?

Lakeland Plastics, a creative kitchenware company, regularly send questionnaires to their mail order customers. An interesting question that they pose is:

Did you feel like complaining about any of our products, but never got round to it? If yes, could we have the chance to put it right now?

Also in market research, Nielsen will place staff actually in the offices and marketing departments of client companies. Accessibility is paramount. Understanding and immediate ability to spot trends, needs and potential problems is the value to Nielsen. Relationship Marketing is all about this type of mutual benefit.

Spend a day in the life of your customers

In an outstanding article in the *Harvard Business Review* (January/February 1994), entitled 'Spend a Day in the Life of Your Customers,' Francis Gouillart and Frederick Sturdivant describe the executive's instinctive capacity to empathise with and gain insights from customers as the single most important skill. Most top-level managers spend time visiting customers. However, their view is that all too often these visits are superficial. The essence of their argument is that this superficial approach focuses on issues across all customers. The commonest issue is price and so, naturally reduced product variety, lower service levels and uniform product designs result. An alternative approach to understand individual customers in depth will have an entirely different outcome. Instead of joining all the other suppliers in moving towards a common pattern of standard ranges, you create particular solutions to needs of individual customers or groups of customers. This added value offering means greater satisfaction and greater customer loyalty.

A first-class example of this approach working is at the Weyerhaeuser sawmill at Cottage Grove, Oregon.

The general manager of the sawmill arranged for a cross-section of employees from himself to the fork lift operator, to spend a week at a time as 'employees' of customers. They were there to look, listen and learn. They returned full of practical ways to make their customers' lives easier. They began colour-coding timber ends, loading lumber in the way that was easiest to unload at the other end. Telephone sales personnel and field staff better understood customer problems, solved and even anticipated them. Buying from Weyerhaeuser was easier and sales rose.

The learning organisation works. Gouillart and Sturdivant conclude, 'Spending a day in the life of the customer is where the real learning occurs.'

Respond to information, respond to changes

The essence of the learning organisation is its responsiveness. Understanding customers and their developing needs is merely the first stage of the model. The second step is the response. As with the Weyerhaeuser example, the responses are small, frequent and numerous. The organisation must respond constantly to myriads of stimuli.

The American Bearings Inc Corporation, wholesalers of indus-
trial bearings, have progressively added motors, drives and belts
to their traditional line-up. They are now conducting energy
audits of factory motors at the plants of their largest customers.

Supervalu Inc, a \$12.6 billion food wholesaler, is cited by
Business Week as making successful initiatives with its retailers,
including financing, staff training and store design. In the UK
motor industry a new information super-highway is opening up
carrying data about new car orders, availability, spare part orders
and warranty information. Recognising the changes and responding rapidly is the answer.

It is all too easy to fail to see the successful potential of new
developments. Let me mention some examples to demonstrate
how easy it is to remain locked in today's assumptions. All the
following instances seemed reasonable at their utterance. Firstly,
in his 'Book of Heroic Failures', Stephen Pile has shown the lack
of vision of Dr Dionysys Lardner (1793–1859), Professor of
Natural Philosophy at University College, London, who declared
that:

> Rail travel at high speed is not possible because passengers, unable
> to breathe, would die of asphyxia.

Two years before the Great Western crossed the Atlantic, the
professor also stated with conviction that:

> No large steamship would be able to cross the Atlantic, because it
> would require more coal than it could carry.

Even IBM, the father of computer companies, once forecast
the world computer market in single figures. In his book *Thriving*

on Chaos, Tom Peters quotes Alan Warner of Warner Brothers on the opportunity for speech in the era of silent movies:

> Who in the hell wants to hear actors talk?

The purpose of these examples of lack of vision is to challenge your current assumptions about what is or is not possible, what people will or will not want. Think the unthinkable!

Perhaps customers of the dairy industry may be right in seeking milk cartons that they can open readily. The years of snackers' frustration with biscuit packs is beginning to close with easy tear tabs only now appearing on a wide scale.

As an exercise, write down three assumptions about change in your industry or business. Save the page of your notebook and review it tomorrow. Are you so certain now?

Following or leading?

The model so far has urged you to gather knowledge of the customer and to respond to that knowledge. This is good. It is not sufficient. Simply responding to customers implies a reactive organisation. An observer and follower of trends. Not a trend-setter. In bygone days, this may have been a successful strategy. Some companies, it is true, can still make this technique work, through their speed and proficiency at reaction. Hewlett Packard, for example, are renowned for their skill in entering new technology second, with more refined answers. Nevertheless, for the majority of organisations, facing a dramatic pace of change, reactivity is not enough.

If you are seeking deep and near permanent relationships with your customers, you have a duty to lead them, not just follow their requests. If you do not know enough to lead the market, perhaps they should be forming their relationships with someone who can.

Anticipate the market

The challenge of management is to understand the market well, better than your customers and competitors, so well, in fact, that you are able to judge which way the market is heading. It is a sensing skill, a talent for discerning trends before they materialise fully. Anticipating the developments of the market allows you to position yourself as the expert and provide the proof every time the trends move on.

How do you anticipate the market?

There are three thoughts which may help your process.

- Look for the lead users in your market.

- Look beyond your own market at more advanced economies.

- Identify the driving influence on your market and observe its direction.

The lead users

Lead users are the customers of your business who are always pressing you to make changes to your products and services to suit their needs, which subsequently turn out to be the needs of a large proportion of your customers. The lead users of Blackpool Pleasure Beach Amusements funfair demanded more frightening roller coaster rides. Now this exists, the majority of trippers are queuing for this sensational experience. Lead users of McDonalds asked for salads ten years ago. Certain rock musicians may be the lead users for guitars and electronic organs. Buyers in Copenhagen often seek services 18 months before the rest of Denmark. You need to understand which are these lead users. Only hindsight identifies them. They were right about the trends. Their requests were followed by bulk orders. You can isolate these users and closely monitor their pressures. Naturally, they are not right in every case. They are right often enough for you to consider their rising expectations seriously. In Japan, Ajinomoto, a big food company, responded to its lead users.

Ajinomoto has supplied Japanese supermarkets with its widening range of food products for many years. They are aware that certain retailers have market foresight, and seek additional services. Instead of directing them to an increasing flow of new product introductions, the pressure is on to boost the appeal of existing products. According to The Economist, *Ajinomoto are now offering computer simulations which predict how a supermarket's sales might change if it stacked its shelves differently.*

Hunt out your lead users. If your sales staff do not know who they are, then the service operation will.

Look beyond your market

The convention on future trends used to be that you that all you needed to do was to take a flight to San Francisco and observe what was happening there. Sadly it is not as simple as that now. There is no single answer any more. Industrial vendors in the People's Republic of China know that they must begin to move from the technical and educational sell towards the more competitive style of other developing South-east Asian markets. Australia leads on some health concerns. France is probably still ahead on perfume trends. Belgian chocolate makers lead the world in confectionary. For advanced automotive technology, the UK's pre-eminence in Grand Prix car design counts for a lot. The management journals and technical magazines in the most advanced markets in your business can tell you a great deal. Translation costs are small compared with the potential upside. Extracted articles may even be available through Internet or at the end of your fax line!

Who influences your customers?

The third technique for anticipating your market is to see the influencers on your customers. This has worked in the most fickle market I know – the toy business. This year's star will be next year's has-been. Yet there is one toy which has thrived at the top of the sales charts for 35 years. It is the Barbie doll.

By early 1994, Mattel toys had sold 775 million Barbie dolls worldwide, with sales operations in 31 countries. Launches planned in further countries include Portugal, Venezuela, China and Argentina. The secret of Barbie's success is the understanding Mattel have of eight-year-old girls. The management know that the people who influence these girls are their twelve-to-fourteen-year-old role models. Mattel researchers patrol amusement parks, shopping malls, skating rinks and anywhere frequented by young teenage girls. They observe the girls with minute attention to detail. What is new? What clothes? What styles? How is their hair? What accessories? What do they discuss? What is important to them? Armed with this up-to-the-minute knowledge, Barbie is constantly refreshed with new outfits, hair styles, companions, equipment, jewellery, footwear and accessories. The successful link with Benetton was a conse-

quence of this understanding. Mattel know where their market is going because they understand its influences.

Innovation and experiment

Even with the help of twelve-year-old role models for Barbie buyers, prediction is a very difficult task. This book began with that thought. To foresee the future of markets is inordinately difficult. Thus the only route is to try new notions, ideas and initiatives. Experiment and innovate. Let the market decide. Sony has devised an exhilarating series of variants of its Walkman. Each has been placed for sale and the judgement of purchasers has determined which models persist and which are deleted.

Unilever Chairman, Michael Perry has made his position clear on innovation. Recently he declared that:

> The battle for competitive edge has moved on: to innovate faster than anyone else. And to roll those innovations, wrapped in perfectly honed brands and positioning around the world. Fast.

There are three fundamental reasons for innovating in our markets (see Figure 7.1). The first derives from Michael Perry's view of reality. It is to hold on to the business we already have. Innovation defends our current sales, perhaps acts as a pre-emptive strike on threatening competitors, and simply keeps us up to date with changing tastes, needs and aspirations. An enhanced clip helps to keep Berol pens ahead of rival Pentel.

The second reason is to widen our margins. This may come through the ever-present pressure for improved value. You may respond with production efficiencies, value engineering and cost savings to lower the price. You may creatively find new angles, benefits and services which justify a premium.

Why innovation?

- TO RETAIN EXISTING BUSINESS
- TO WIDEN MARGINS
- TO WIN NEW BUSINESS

Fig 7.1 Three reasons for innovation

Häagen-Dazs, for example . . .

The Häagen-Dazs plants in France and the United States certainly produce ice cream efficiently and operate with minimal head count and carefully controlled overheads. That is the style of a company owned by Grand Metropolitan plc. However the thrust of the Häagen-Dazs developments is not to lower prices. On the contrary, since Grand Met acquired Pillsbury, which included Häagen-Dazs – a luxury brand of ice cream sold in New York since the mid 1960s – their efforts have been directed at enhancing its quality with luxurious and indulgent ingredients. A few cents of Almond Crunch can put half a dollar on the list price. Now sold in more than twenty major markets in Europe, Asia and the Americas, it is an example of creativity in developing markets and widening margins.

Winning new business – four different ways

The third reason for innovation is to win new business (see Figure 7.2). It is to open up new markets, as Sega and Nintendo have done with computer console games, as Cable & Wireless have done with mobile telephones. Or to discover new and attractive segments, as Avon Cosmetics are doing geographically in China, as Sony achieved with the under-eights age group and My First

Sony. Or to increase usage among existing customers, like Kelloggs with the anytime appeal of their breakfast cereals, like Swatch who persuaded customers that watches were a fashion accessory and they need new models to co-ordinate with changing styles. Or to take business off your competitors, like General Motors with the Omega in Europe and Saturn in the United States, like Gillette with their Sensor shaving range.

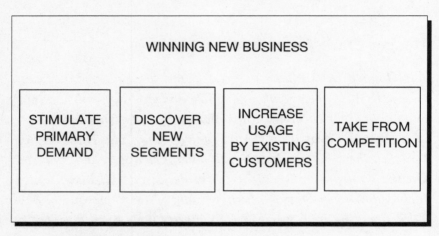

Fig 7.2 Winning new business

Who benefits from innovation?

Simply stated, everyone benefits. Naturally customers benefit from a better product, service, or improved value and performance. The company benefits from increased turnover and greater customer loyalty. This increases morale, motivation, possibly rewards and maybe job security for employees and management. Shareholders gain from dividends, capital appreciation and the comfort of retaining shares rather than the inconvenience of selling to gain better performance elsewhere. On a wider scale, suppliers may have orders extended, contractors benefit from additional work directly, like haulage, and indirectly with affordability of projects and developments. Distributors and dealers benefit from extra turnover. Industrial customers may be able to offer further services downstream to their customers. The community will benefit from tax revenues, the effect of employee and company expenditure locally.

Success and failure

For successful innovation, there is a virtuous circle, whereby benefits extend in a wider ripple to impact on a large number of individuals. Not all innovations are successful. However (again from 'Thriving on Chaos' by Tom Peters) as Soichiro Honda of the eponymous car company said,

> Success can only be achieved through repeated failure and introspection. In fact success represents the 1 per cent of your work, which results *only* from the 99 per cent that is called failure.

Without failure there is no success. The Wright brothers only achieved sustained powered human flight with 805 tries.

Resistance to change

Many resist change simply because of its risk element. The danger of failure is always there. Some personalities are risk averse. You do not reach the top of many professions by deliberate risk-taking! Yet the act of standing fast is a risk in its own right. Makers of reel-to-reel tape recorders, steam locomotives and milk churns are testimony to that risk. In every organisation, there are legitimate and practical reasons against hasty change. For example, the assets of a company are decreased by the premature scrapping of plant. Range complexity is a cost and obsolete products may have to be discounted. There are also emotional and human pretexts against it. Try superseding the line introduced by the managing director! You will always find a member of the sales team opposed to a range deletion, or an update which removes one customer's favourite feature.

Yet change, we must

The business of business is change. It is an essential component. There is no perfect point at which all this change can stop and we have time to digest it. The process continues. A brand manager must appreciate that 'brand' is a verb. Think of it as an active and on-going process. 'Brand', as a noun is a statuesque piece of history. Christopher Lorenz of the *Financial Times* has written that the greatest virtue of a firm is its 'restless questioning'. The feeling is that you may never relax. You may never feel comfortable with now, and how things are. You should always be testing, exploring and enquiring how things could be made better.

Business is an art

Testing and experimenting results in answers to problems. The first answer is not always the only or the right answer. In one important dimension business is an art form. Science teaches us that there is a single correct answer. Twelve times three is always thirty-six. Yellow and blue light combine to form green. In art there is no single correct answer. A statue of the Virgin Mary by one sculptor is a stimulus to the next, whose interpretation may inspire future artists in stone. The first sketch of a painting may lead to twenty more and three successive versions of the final canvass. Each benefits in some way from the increasing expertise of the painter. So it is with innovation. The first answer is a stimulus to devise further and more inspirational concepts. Her idea is a springboard for your improvement and his refinement.

Learning in practice

We all have our favourite examples of ideas implemented successfully in practice. Sometimes these are the springboard for our own businesses. Perhaps you can refine one of these.

Product ideas

Customers buy products for their functional performance and often emotional considerations. Research and analysis often concentrate on the rational, particularly in business-to-business markets. It is of course right to focus first on improving the actual performance of the motor, cleaner or whatever. Without leading edge performance, no amount of psychology and relationship building will suffice. It is the beginning. It is part of the unwritten contract between company and customer that in return for loyalty, the customer will never be out of date through that loyalty. Gillette are the arch exponents of this pace of updating to crush opposition.

Benetton, the Italian manufacturer of bright wool garments, regard their 7,000 retail shops and franchisees as their customers. For these customers, speed in delivery and responsiveness to changes in fashionable colours means that the Benetton priority lies in an automated warehouse operation. The flexibility is achieved with innovative simplicity. Garments are produced in grey and dyed appropriately prior to dispatch.

The essence of product improvement is a close picture of how customers select, use and react with the product. How do they grip the toothbrush handle, and can you increase comfort? How do they judge the comfort and style of an office chair, and can you educate them or work within their expectations?

However, beyond the laboratory approach of logical Research and Development engineers, there is a world of illogicality with a rational explanation. For example, in consumer markets, the first action with a newly purchased mattress is to cover it with bed clothes. The pattern on the mattress is invisible, yet that design and colour style will have a huge impact on the success or failure of a technically excellent mattress. Likewise in the motor industry, Unipart take pains with the paint finish on their silencer and exhaust systems. Customers prefer a good appearance. Strange, since the paint burns off on the first journey the new system makes! But Unipart well understands its customers. Radiators, as part of a cental heating system, are sold painted in primer, as they will be repainted in gloss to match the house interior decor. One manufacturer displayed true enterprise when they revised the shade of primer from brilliant white (a little cold), to a barely detectable pinky white (a little warmer). Sales to hard-bitten builders merchants and building tradesmen soared by 30 per cent.

Products can be enhanced by scents and smells. According to the *New Scientist*, the smell of new-mown grass deliberately wafted through Selfridges gardening department substantially boosts sales among gardeners. Food retailers use the smell of fresh ground coffee and new-baked bread to great effect. Beyond these obvious examples, Shiseido have found in clinical trials that a certain scent enhanced the performance of a stress-reducing drug. A soothing aroma added personal conviction to the chemical efficacy of the compound. Smell carries its disadvantages too. Another Japanese company had to change the scent in a cleaning aerosol which was reminiscent of a lavatory cleaner of the 1940s and thus rejected unconsciously by older users.

National preferences for certain fragrances can be conflicting. In some markets lemon is freshness. In others, it has to be pine.

Colours too can be deceptive. The meaning of a colour in one culture may be absent or contrary in other cultures. The Dutch affection for orange relates to their royal house of Orange. Death is signified by black in some Western countries, where white and purple carry that loading in other cultures.

The packaging counts too

Colour has a big impact on packaging, which is another key area of attention when looking for that beneficial innovation. Crown Berger Paints looked hard at both retailer and customer needs when they redesigned the cans containing their paint.

With the retailer in mind Crown Berger created a squared container from PET which had rounded corners. In this way they could deliver the greatest litrage per metre of shelf space – greater than round cans. The seal was improved to minimise in shop spills (and car-boot spills on the way home from the store, for which retailers were also blamed!) and the label clarity enhanced. For the customer the handle was placed slightly off centre so that the handyman decorating his or her home could coat the brush without covering the handle in the process.

In the UK snacks market, salted peanuts are a major component. The brand leader, KP Nuts, identified packaging as an opportunity when they determined to enliven the product's performance.

Close observation of customers by KP Nuts had illustrated the different segments and their different needs. For out and about snacking by younger people, accessibility into the packs was the problem. Ripping the packs sprayed nuts everywhere. A new and

*patented drum design with plastic lid eliminated the problem
with flair. Growth became dynamic. For older consumers who
bought larger packs for home consumption over a number of
days or even weeks, the concern was retaining freshness. The
bigger pack was redesigned to have a flat base to prevent open
bags falling over, and a ground coffee type reseal tape was added
to the specification. Similar success resulted.*

Innovative service makes a difference too

Success can be derived from service initiatives. One of the UK's
foremost retailers, now present in Europe and Hong Kong, is
Marks & Spencer.

*Marks & Spencer chilled food in the form of prepared meals has
won recognition to the extent that in some quarters it is acceptable to present these at a dinner party. To confirm this trend and
to add wine sales to the portfolio, Marks & Spencer are testing
an interactive terminal allowing shoppers to specify number of
guests and courses. It then advises them of ideal food and wine
combinations and suggested quantities.*

Renault have understood that the fundamental need addressed
by a motor car is reliable mobility. You expect to be able to go
where you want, when you want.

*Renault dealers had already attended to the provision of a
replacement vehicle during services and mechanical repairs. The
manufacturer had designed the vehicle range to have short times
in the service bay. There was another step forward. Drivers lose
this reliable mobility when they are involved in an accident. Into*

the breach steps Renault Accident Management. Originally offered to business fleets only, it is now extended to private users. A 24-hour free-phone number is called and from then on Renault manages, controls and pursues the whole recovery and repair procedure from start to finish. They eliminate post crash hassles and reduce trauma. They also promise a speedier return to mobility, with an average of ten days off the road, compared with the average of twenty days.

Hertz, whose business may be marginally jeopardised by this type of initiative, are tackling their potential markets with enthusiasm. To encourage hirers to extend the period beyond the minimum business requirement, they now encourage pleasure motoring. Three or four times a year they produce a touring magazine for the glove box. This contains a variety of bright and informative suggestions for places to visit, complete with a set of maps to assist in locating the venues.

Information through customer magazines

Many organisations use the knowledge they possess of their products, markets and customers, to devise customer magazines. Using magazines it is possible to segment precisely. Rover Cars innovated with a multi-topic format with selective binding, so that customers could choose from a menu of article types. Everyone received the motor section, of course, but some elected for travel, where others specified gardening. In the 1980s TSB Bank's growth was stimulated by a segmented portfolio of customer magazines.

TSB Bank – steered by Advertising Manager, Roger Linn – developed and refined TSBeat, a termly magazine for 13 to 15 year olds, mailed in bulk direct to the majority of secondary schools in the UK. This featured articles explaining banking in very accessible terms. Other features captured youth interest and engendered response through competitions, offers and correspondence pages. High levels of interaction occurred. During this time TSB Bank had the largest share of youth account wins among its competitors. Next came Yes Magazine, *aimed squarely at bank customers and potential customers from their 20s to their late 40s. This was the helpful guide to financial matters, full of hints, advice and checklists for money major decisions. The accent was on lead generation – more than 50,000 per issue – many of which were successfully converted by branch staff. Finally a magazine aimed at retired people covered investments among other matters of general and financial interest.*

Magazines for customers can build loyalty successfully, though success depends on patience and commitment. Success does not appear with the first issue. Further examples from Benetton, Microsoft and IBM will be discussed in Chapter 9. Magazines also add value to membership clubs.

Join the Club

A regular newsletter is a central plank in the JOS Club, run by Jardine Office Services of Hong Kong. The aim of the club is to support customers and help them stay up-to-date with the developments in office technology. Regular customers are awarded membership which provides help line support, priority booking for places at product seminars and invitations to pre-launch briefings of up-grades.

Promotional flair can help

The learning organisation will learn, not simply how to improve loyalty through better products, services and support, but also how better to attract attention with promotional ideas. Creativity can create impact here too. A further example from Hong Kong is the Nike promotion.

Nike, to reinforce their lifestyle appeal, created 'Just Do It' Real Life Triumph Awards. In the words of the promotion leaflet, 'They said you couldn't. No way. But you did it. Let's hear it.' Prizes for achievement and overcoming adversity included the JDI trophy, five-day trips to Japan and the chance to meet basketball whiz, Michael Jordan. The headline captured the Nike message completely – 'Dear Nike, I'm 80 and I swam the harbour naked!'

Charities face ever-increasing pressures to attract donations, and innovative approaches work equally well here. Innovators frequently think of ways to 'fish further upstream' of rivals. Many charities offer opportunities to travellers to donate their unconvertible foreign coins at airports and ports. Now the United Nations Children's Fund, UNICEF, has gone upstream.

UNICEF, in conjunction with British Airways, have launched 'Change for Good'. Lasting until 1997, cabin crews on long-haul flights will collect unwanted foreign coins and notes donated by passengers who will have just seen the UNICEF video on the in-flight entertainment system.

Creativity is often simply a matter of reframing the ways things have been done previously, and adding pieces of reinforcement, like the in-flight video. Certainly organisational learning is vital to keep faith with the expectations of your loyal customers.

And is it working?

The experimentation and innovation is only half the story. The other aspect is the reaction of your customers to the innovation. Like the waiter/waitress in the best restaurants, you are always there, unobtrusively checking that all is well. The next phase of the model for the learning organisation is to seek feedback constantly.

At Ashridge Management College, close to 4000 managers are trained each year across a wide spectrum of industries, issues and programmes. Yet every manager completes a detailed satisfaction survey including session by session commentaries, views on pedagogical approaches, catering standards, reception and every other service provided. The completed reviews go immediately to the dean of the college and are a fundamental part of the continuous development that takes place in practical educational approaches and support services.

Are you seeking feedback constantly, or are you relying on the vociferous to represent the views of the majority? Personal visits to customers are one way, as commended by Gouillart and Sturdivant in the *Harvard Business Review* (January/February 1994) article 'Spend a Day in the Life of Your Customers'. Telephone calls are another. Inviting customers to visit you will provide further feedback. Tracking of satisfaction with service initiatives is well developed. Pursue both formal and informal approaches. Ask questions. Observe. Listen. If you are very senior in your organisation, force the system to give you honest feedback. Best of all, ask the customer yourself.

Key customer reviews

In industrial markets, you will ensure that you hold regular reviews with key customers. Preferably at their premises the agenda will address all the issues impacting on the relationship. My suggestion is that the first item on the agenda should always be, what is new in the business? This way you will begin on a positive note and tackle your mutual need for insight into the future when you are fresh. Tackle the minutiae of problem solving subsequently.

Your role – Guide to your customers

In markets which are constantly evolving and developing, your customers have a need beyond their product and service needs. It is a need for reassurance and support. They want allies and partners who can guide them through the succession of radical changes. The concept of Relationship Marketing places you firmly as that guide.

SUMMARY

• Being a learning organisation is an essential part of Relationship Marketing. Learning means knowing and understanding your customers. It includes responding to their unfolding needs, and foreseeing these needs before them. Experiments, pilots and tests are an important ingredient so that your product or service reflects latest developments. Constantly seek feedback so you know that your initiatives are on the right track for customers. You owe it to the purchasers who are investing their custom in a long-term relationship with you, to provide them with a state of the art product. Never over-specified. Always meeting needs. No

amount of relationship building and customer involvement makes up for under-developed products. Relationships are built on confidence. Your customers must have
the confidence that you are the expert. You can only be
that expert if you – as an organisation – are continuously
learning.

8

RELATIONSHIP PRICING

It is true for personal and commercial relationships that the greatest potential for quarrels and disagreements is money. The financial dimensions of a relationship are the most fraught with risk. The pricing aspect of Relationship Marketing is crucial. This chapter examines the threats and opportunities that price offers within the commercial relationship.

What is price?

The price in a transaction is the balance point between the interests of the two parties. In its simplest terms it may represent the lowest figure the vendor is prepared to accept for parting with his item, and the highest amount the purchaser is prepared to pay. Scarcity, availability of substitutes and ability to manage without the item will all be taken into account. In this way it is an economist's medium of exchange.

Price in marketing terms also connotes value. Thus the position of a product in the choice dimension will be influenced by the list price. Aspects like exclusivity and status are heavily influenced by the price. Lower prices, in principle, imply higher volumes and lower exclusivity. This is not always the case. Swatch, for example, represent relatively high status for their price band through the device of managed scarcity. To buy the Swatch you like you must hurry as it will only be available in limited quantities.

Price is also an important determinant of profit performance. Too high and volumes suffer hitting profit. Too low and margins are inadequate to provide the necessary returns. Too sudden in their movements up or down and customers and shareholders lose confidence in the management.

Price setting

There are three points in the price setting process. These are shown in Figure 8.1.

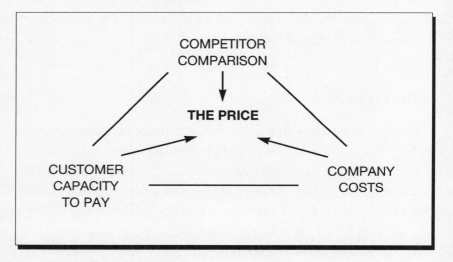

Fig 8.1 The price setting process

The simplest and worst approach to price setting is to consider internal costs, apply an adequate mark-up and publish this as a list price. The marginally more demanding approach is to gather competitor price lists and to set prices in relation to these competitors. Thus, the position would be below a superior product and above an apparently inferior product. In this way whole markets can move together away from customer opportunities. The appropriate approach is to look primarily at the value to the customer of the product and its affordability to the buying organisation. Comparisons with competitors are a cross check. Internally the question must be, how can we make it for the price the customer is prepared to pay.

The essence of Relationship Marketing is that prices should be driven by understanding the customer. Prices charged must reflect the learning that has taken place in the relationship.

And maybe prices will fall . . .

The new dynamic factor, mentioned earlier, is the concept of falling prices. In many markets, prices do not need to rise at all. If world inflation remains near its current levels, technology, creativity and efficiency can bring down prices steadily. The consumer cost of a telephone call can fall lower and lower. The Belgian phone monopoly premium is under threat. Where costs do not fall, value can accelerate. Motor car tyres offer 30 times the life in use that they gave only 60 years ago. With readily available labour, capital and raw materials (or substitutes), we are in for a period of value enhancement.

Retail customers will receive these benefits. Retail brands must work to deliver these benefits. Companies supplying other businesses must consider how to ensure their customers can receive and pass on these benefits.

To encapsulate this, price has to effect a transaction without acrimony, deliver profit to the vendor (and the purchaser if there is on-selling), and communicate the right messages, during a period of price variability. Challenges indeed.

The value of Relationship Marketing

In the third chapter, we saw the increase in profitability which could result from long lasting relationships. The benefits came from less spent in customer acquisition, increased volume over time, lower costs from dealing with a familiar organisation and new business from referrals. These benefits to the vendor's margins represent a potential conflict from the buyer's perspective.

Conflict in an otherwise harmonious partnership

How can two parties feel so differently about part of the relationship? They can agree on product specification, after-sales service, technical support, means of communication, delivery logistics the staff with whom they have regular contact and so on. They have an interest in resolving all of these to their mutual benefit. Yet it seems that price does not work in the same way. The perception is that in this dimension only:

> Your gain is my loss and
> my gain is at your expense.

Overcoming this potential relationship-busting threat is the role of relationship pricing.

Three rules of relationship pricing

- Share the benefit with your long-term customers.
- Never use price as a promotional weapon.
- Develop customer-based prices.

Rule 1: Share the sweeties

The benefit of Relationship Marketing is that you trade more efficiently with long-time customers and therefore less cost is consumed by inefficiencies. If these benefits are shared with customers, they receive better value which ensures they have another incentive to remain loyal. It should represent a virtuous circle.

The norm in many businesses is that the additional profitability from loyal customers is allocated to fund competitive offers to attract new customers. When a bank promotes itself to students with three year competitive prices which equate to operating losses, then someone else is funding that. Resentment is caused and trust breaks down.

The way to share the benefits of stability of business is different in consumer and industrial markets.

Consumer markets – reward loyalty with extra value. In consumer markets the motion is relatively straightforward. It consists of lower prices or better value. The latter is preferable from the organisational point of view. Rather than lowering the price, you give extra support to the regular buyers – advice and guidance, rewards related to the product, free stock of new lines for assessment. Heinz is looking at ways of reaching families and other groups consuming high volumes of its products. Clubs joined by purchase qualification give a means of sharing the benefits of loyalty with the loyal fraternity.

Consumer markets – do not reward loyalty with lower prices. Greater value tends to be appreciated and builds loyalty. Lower prices tend to be forgotten, so the brand does not receive the recognition due. There is a retail marketing abbreviation, KPI. This is a 'Known Price Item', a product where a large number of buyers have an accurate recall of its normal selling price. The average supermarket will sell more than 40,000 lines. Few surveys find more than a score of KPIs. While you are price competitive with comparative products, always select better value routes over price cutting.

However, your category may be out of line on price. Your study of comparative products must include a wide selection embracing the direct alternative and acceptable substitutes. Chips, potato waffles, bread and pasta all compete with rice. If your whole category – say rice – is over-priced then action must be taken, irrespective of the price position of your rice brand rivals.

In an industrial market – you give consultancy. Your approach is different and you will aim to apply your knowledge of your customers and your products and services to help make them more profitable. Forget that you are a supplier of gas, or vat cleaners, or paint or trucks. Imagine you are an expert consultant paid on the strength of the improvement the customer can make to profit.

Help your customers make more money, don't give it to them. This could be in the form of increased volume sales. It might be through increased margins on the strength of a better product, or lower cost of production. It might even be through the customer's ability to command greater loyalty in that marketplace. The aim is to reward the loyalty you have received with a benefit which enables the customer to make greater returns. You may actually invest quite heavily in your business to extend these benefits to your customer. It might in the short time frame, have been cheaper to give an extra 5 per cent discount. In the long run, the message that I am investing substantially to build your business is a cogent defence of loyalty. See the mutual benefit.

Rule 2: Never use price as a promotional weapon

Price promotions:

- Start price wars which every-one loses.

- Damage the value image you have built up.

- Teach customers to await the next offer.

- Create expensive demand surges.

- Lead to subsequent demand collapses.

- Disrupt your customers stock levels.

- Given to new customers anger existing customers.

- Imply you have stock problems.

- Suggest you may be replacing the line.

- Exaggerate your perceived profit margins.

- Generate stock outs.

- Distract your staff from customer needs.

- Invalidate employee performance measurements.

- Confuse sales trend analysis.

  Take price out of the equation.
  The ideal stance has three sections:

1 The product, its service, support and reliability offers compelling benefits. (moderate emphasis)

2 The price is fair. (low emphasis)

3 A final benefit, perhaps of personalisation, or representing innovation. (high emphasis)

The retail proponents of this style are the UK departmental store group, John Lewis, whose carrier bags bear the reassuring slogan:

NEVER KNOWINGLY UNDERSOLD

You have experienced a helpful and understanding sales process. You have bought the product. The communication implies that you have carried out the transaction at a fair price. The price worry is taken away, to permit you to focus on the product and its performance.

The contrast is with the Kingfisher Group, whose strategy of 'Every Day Low Prices' at Woolworths has appeared less successful. The message puts low prices at the top of the agenda. Is the only reason for coming to the store the fact that it has cheap prices? Are there no product or service or pleasure benefits?

Rule 3: Develop customer-based prices

The elementary marketing theory of needs explains that when a customer buys a Rolex, he does not want a time-piece, he is seeking a means to display his status. When a customer buys a Swatch, she wants a fashionable accessory, rather than a wrist-based time display.

The driver does not want a bucket and a sponge for their intrinsic merit – the need is for a clean car.

Relationship pricing understands this concept and applies it.

In Manchester an enterprising vehicle valeting and car wash company, began selling 'clean cars'. For £250, you can have a clean car for a year. No one counts the number of times the car comes in for a shampoo. The driver is not seeking a single car wash for £5.00. If around the block, the car comes under the flight path of incontinent pigeons, splashes through muddy puddles and chocolate melts on the seat, back it goes for a further clean. The need is for a clean vehicle.

The same principle applies to business to business markets. The *Harvard Business Review* of January/February 1994, in an article by Gouillart and Sturdivant, cites Nalco Chemical of Illinois.

Nalco Chemical provide chemical water treatment services for industrial operations like steel mills, oil refineries and paper mills. Originally they sold chemicals by the drum. Actually, their customers did not want drums of chemicals, they wanted clean water. Now, Nalco Chemical run a service operation, guaranteeing the best available handling of water treatment issues. They charge a fee for a service, not a price for the drum.

Both examples illustrate that pricing can be more powerful if it is customer based. What is the customer seeking? How can you provide this performance at the lowest possible cost for the customer?

The premise is that you are the expert. Rather than using the expertise to sell the product, why not sell what the customer needs for a fee and include the product used within that fee. It would be possible to sell water treatment chemicals in a greater concentration than the customer actually needs. Perhaps a cautious customer rounds up the quantity specified to be safe. Perhaps the customer takes three different chemicals, as a compromise, when six precisely measured compounds would cover the treatments accurately for a lower cost. By delivering the lowest cost guaranteed pure water, the chemical company is taking cost out of the buyer's business, removing a technical requirement for the buyer's staff and giving the priceless promise of peace of mind. An itinerant pedlar of cheap drums of chemicals could never displace Nalco.

What result does your customer want?

Ask yourself, what result does my customer want? The client of an advertising agency is not after a 30-second blockbuster with the brand name as finale. The client wants a payback, which might be the ability to command higher prices from a stronger image. It might be a sales increase. Should the agency be paid for delivering that payback? The real application of customer-based pricing is to ask the client for a fee of 4 per cent of the value of the additional sales. Most agencies and clients shy away from the negotiation. Imagine how differently client and agent would behave if the rewards were structured in this way. The client has the security of knowing the advertising costs as a proportion of sales value. The advertising judgement is not emotive and based on likes or dislikes. The risk and responsibility is shared with the agency. The agency has a dramatic bottom line interest in value for money. The lower the cost of delivering the client's target, the more profit the agency achieves. Where agencies are currently remunerated on advertising commission, their interests are best served by increasing expenditure. It is a big step. A medium-sized step would be for client and agency to agree to calculate the notional impact had they operated in that fashion in the year past.

Customer profitability

To operate on this new basis, the supplier must cost every single part of the service on a per customer basis. Only with a complete understanding of the costs of supplying and servicing that customer can a correct calculation be undertaken of the right price to charge. There must be no cost camouflage, cross-subsidies and hidden mysteries.

Tyre companies flying ahead

In one industry, this has already happened. Airlines formerly bought their aeroplane tyres in bulk at a price per tyre. No longer. They are in the passenger and cargo transportation business, not the science of rubber compounds matched to weights, air temperature and atmospheric pressure. The airline now buys a tyre service. It owns no tyres, has no stock, no responsibility for tyre pressures, wear monitoring, profile or compound specification. The tyre company manages the total process. With their knowledge, they can maximise tyre life, minimise stock holding and deliver a complete service. The results are mutually beneficial. The airline can cost its tyres on the same basis as its meals, virtually on a per passenger ratio. Thus it understands the cost structure of its business better. In fact the service costs less than when they bought the tyres and managed the service. The tyre company has a security of business and learns more about its own product than any laboratory could offer.

The final step

The next extension beyond customer-based pricing is open book accounting. The partnership between the two companies is so close, that the supplier charges cost price for the service, all invoices, cost calculations and allocations shown. In return the supplier is able to levy an agreed management charge. In this way two companies can explore the cost base mutually and jointly discover cost savings. With an understanding of the supply costs, the buyer may be able to alter the specification to agree a new standard, which performs as well for a lower cost.

SUMMARY

- The importance of price to both buyer and seller's profitability throws a particular stress on this aspect of Relationship Marketing. At the same time, technological developments and world competition are pressuring price levels in many markets. The risks of price problems in the relationship can be addressed with three rules.

1   Share the benefit with your long term customers.

2   Never use price as a promotional weapon.

3   Develop customer based prices,

9

CUSTOMER COMMUNICATIONS

A relationship begins with a conversation, and continuing communication maintains and sustains it. Therefore, in Relationship Marketing, communication is critical for success. We are born with two ears and a single mouth; this is a guide to the balance of our communications. Listen first, to learn from your market. Speak, and listen again for the feedback. Dialogue with customers keeps the commercial relationship flourishing.

Interactive communication

The objective of a company's communications is to assist in the building of long-term and continuous relationships. Effective interactive communication is essential to maintain the mutual understanding which is the basis of Relationship Marketing. This chapter is about successful interactive communication.

Audience, message and media

Achieving the company's communications' objectives depends on three factors: the right audience, the right message and the right media. The right audience or audiences will be clear from the customer understanding covered in Chapter 7 – The learning organisation. The understanding must of course be shared with communicators and agencies involved. Better still, those employed to craft the communications should have their own opportunity to watch, listen and study individuals in the audience. Reportedly, Unilever dress dummies in clothing typical of the detergent's users and place these figures in the rooms where creativity is taking place, as a reminder of the target audience. In the 1980s Peter Taylor, then Marketing Director for Trumans Brewery, had a large portrait of a typical drinker on the wall of his office in his direct line of sight. The message too comes from the understanding of the customer, and also the detailed picture of the product and the need it addresses in the life of the purchaser.

The message design in addition acknowledges competitor activity. The communication must convey distinct messages to the customer which are different from those of rivals in the market. The communications convey the positioning of the company, product or service. These must be relevant to the audience, realistic and convincing.

Understanding the company (products/services)	Understanding customers	Understanding competitors
Realistic communication	Relevant and convincing communications	Differentiated communications

There are guidelines for communicating messages successfully. These follow. Then we shall look at media routes to achieve the communications objectives.

Communication strategy

In Chapter 2, we looked at the parallels between personal communications and the commercial communications between organisations. Using the thesis that there is a common basis, consider how an individual might respond if the relationship with their partner is threatened by a third party aiming to win the partner away. The intuitive response would be to increase communications rather than reduce them, to attempt to make communication even more personal, to be consistent and to hit the right note. These natural reactions form the basis for the communication strategy of the organisation.

Frequency

Firstly, the most important part of the communications strategy is to ensure that communication is sufficiently frequent. More customers are lost through lack of follow up, and what appears to the customer to be indifference, than any other cause of lost sales. What is 'frequent'?

Frequent is most likely to mean more frequent than competitors. A study of competitor communications may indicate real opportunities for you to get closer to customers. Uncover the customer feelings about your own communication patterns and those of your rivals.

Competitor approaches are variable. My suggestion is that a strategy should be based on customer defined expectations. Simply ask customers how often they would like you to be in touch.

A major multi-country charitable organisation relies for a valuable portion of its income upon individual wealthy donors who make sizeable personal donations regularly. These philanthropists are most important for their contributions to funds and also for their influence on others. Often they are important figures in their community, and promote the cause of the charity. For both these reasons, it is appropriate and courteous to keep them informed on the activities and results of the charity's initia-

tives. This might include regular income and expenditure reports, regional activity plans, news of headquarter initiatives, details of forthcoming events, problems envisaged, linkages with commercial organisations and sponsorships. One approach would be to provide these philanthropists with all the available information. Another would be to select specific reports for them. The best solution is simply to give them a menu of available information and allow them to choose what they wish to see and how frequently they wish to be contacted.

Asking donors how often they wish to be contacted is a developing standard in the field of charity marketing. It is a neat and polite way to minimise donor fatigue and maximise postal cost efficiencies. People who have specified a six-monthly cycle are also more likely to make a donation twice a year, because they were party to this contact plan. It may be that charity marketers are ahead of their profit sector colleagues in this aspect of relationship building.

A final word on communication frequency is to stay watchful. Competitor initiatives come and go. New standards emerge. Expectations of customers change. Keep in touch on how often to keep in touch.

Make it personal

The second precept is to make communications more individual, so that they have a feeling of personalisation. Already we have touched on how customer choice of frequency builds a relationship. Similarly, further ways for customers to specify their personal requirements are an important part of the communications approach. Choosing your own shade of wall paint and seeing it mixed while you wait is proof of your individuality. The campaign for Burger King, 'Have it your way', is all about respecting customer preferences and allowing you to tailor a standard offering through exercising choices. The Body Shop even make a purchase personal with a question.

When you buy your hair shampoo, you are asked whether you need a carrier bag. This tiny question is full of meaning. It gives you an element of choice. Either way you have added your preference to the process. You are involved. More than this, the question reminds you of the Body Shop's commitment to sustainability of world resources. Their differentiation from other vendors of beauty products is this environmental concern. Letting you choose not to have a bag that you will subsequently discard encourages you to buy into and reinforce their competitive advantage. Note that it is an invitation to support their view, not a pressure.

Personalisation comes in many forms. Ultimately it is the bespoke design, unique in the globe, made only for you. The gradations take you all the way to a mass produced pack of chewing gum, served with a smile and a momentary individual piece of eye contact.

Are three billion people wrong?

Perception is all. How does the customer feel? If the answer is that he or she felt like the hundredth transaction that day in a uniform year of business, then there is no personalisation. Worse, there is the implied insult – you are just like everyone else. Three billion people on this Earth believe that they are not just like everyone else. Are three billion people wrong?

I don't have to out-run the bear . . .

Perception is also relative. There is an old tale often recounted at sales conferences, especially in the sports footwear industry:

Two Canadian campers were disturbed by the roar of an angry grizzly bear, heading towards them. One immediately rushed to don his Nike/Adidas/Cica/Reebok/Hi-Tech trainers (select brand according to conference!). 'Don't be ridiculous', his companion shouted, 'you will never out-run the bear!' The first retorted, 'I don't have to out-run the bear, I just have to out run you!'

In other words, it is not necessary for your product or service to be the acme of individualisation. This is probably unaffordable in production and over-specifying the market. It simply needs to be perceived as more individual than the rival brands.

Consistent success from consistent behaviour

Not only do consumers want to be treated as individuals, they also see the selling organisation as an individual. They imbue your firm with the personality characteristics of an individual. They expect that individual to act with consistency. How disconcerting it is when the friendly person you know greets you with a frown. How puzzling when the chatterbox is silent. How irritating when the humble supplicant displays arrogance. Organisations can unwittingly display dual personalities.

Consistency of approach is a norm for customers. When the organisation acts 'out of character', the buyer may well not consciously understand the basis of their frustration. They only know that they have been surprised by the unexpected behaviour. If this is an unpleasant surprise, the reaction is likely to be emotional retreat from the previous relationship. The consequence of this depends on the depth of the relationship. When a life-long friend behaves oddly, you may well make allowances, and will certainly give them another chance. When a shallow acquaintance gives you a nasty surprise, the likelihood is that this will damage the relationship thereafter. So it is with organisational relationships.

Consistency is most easily displayed or shattered through organisational communications. The computer store advertises expert advice and guidance in stark contrast with the Neanderthal ignorance of the unhelpful assistant. The avuncular friendliness oozed by the book club, conflicts directly with the curt questions fired by the credit accounts supervisor. The organisation at odds with itself is conveyed adroitly in a Video Arts training film, where the service engineer for a household appliance manufacturer disloyally demands, 'Who sold you this then?' The strong message is that the company sales staff should not have sold that model to that customer. One organisation, two contradictory messages.

Take as your model for consistency, a daily newspaper. Consistency is not like the words of an epic poem, fixed for all time. Longfellow's poem, 'The Village Blacksmith', always begins with:

> Under a spreading chestnut tree
> The village smithy stands;
> The smith, a mighty man is he,
> With large and sinewy hands.

Every day a newspaper begins with different words. Its lead story will change daily, sometimes even altering between editions on the same day. All major newspapers have their own character. So each day a newspaper crafted from new words must reflect the unique character, values and style conceived to meet the expectations of the regular readership.

The character and values will not vacillate from one day to the next, but are sure to adapt and respond to political change and social mores. The style can flex more frequently with currents of fashion. New words come into vogue, technical advances give greater opportunities to editors. Thus the newspaper is a living model of consistency for its readers, while it grows and develops with their own developing thinking.

The newspaper creates a perception of consistency. A newspaper which remained rigid in its approaches over time would seem to have ossified. Its readers – not seeing their own progress – would feel that it had slipped back in time. It is the same way for organisations. Their personalities must present a clear identity, but not allow themselves to become locked at a point in time.

Hitting the right note

Finally, the communications must achieve the right tone of voice. The communications need to be in keeping with the organisation's image, and in addition they must have a style appropriate and acceptable to their audience. The simplest example is the button you press to operate your photocopier. 'START' is an instruction to you, an authoritative order from company to customer. In contrast, 'READY' implies willingness and availability for service from the firm to the customer. The conscious mind does not set itself against the photocopier manufacturer whose button reads 'START', but subconsciously the warmth and helpfulness is not there. The firm has missed an opportunity to hit the right note.

UCI Cinemas hit the right note when they ran a promotion in early 1994, with prizes of Virgin Atlantic flights to the United States of America or the Far East. The excellent copy-writer obviously spent time in cinemas appreciating the promotion readership. Public recognition is relevant to a film-goer – so the copy highlighted UCI's status as Cinema Chain of the Year 1993, and Virgin's accolade of Airline of the Year 1993 (for the third year running). Knowledge of the audience shone through with the introduction to the terms and conditions:

> Please read the terms and conditions – we *know* they are boring, but they are there to help you understand the promotion fully, and to prevent any disappointment.

The tone of voice is appropriate, so appropriate in fact that the cinema-goer reading those words would feel at one with UCI. He or she would notice nothing unusual about the promotion, but be inclined to enter. If prompted, the response might be that UCI are on the same wavelength as me. No dissonance occurs where the communication hits the right note.

COMMUNICATION CHECKLIST

- **Interactive. Listen, speak, listen for feedback.**
- **Frequent. Let the customer define frequency.**
- **Personalised. Relative to rivals, does it feel more individual?**
- **Consistent. Is it always in character?**
- **Tone of voice. Is it striking the right note?**

These approaches then are the guidelines for the organisation's communication strategy. Having looked at audiences and messages, we now turn to the media to achieve the communications aims.

The media

A number of ways of maintaining relationships while geographically separated were listed in Chapter 2. Using this as a structure we shall look at the communications media which could be deployed.

Firstly, however, let us look at paid advertising. It is the first port of call for many organisations. Television still has the largest share of global advertising revenue, though there are now hundreds of other choices, from phone-card advertising and slogans on bus-sides, to screens built into supermarket shopping trolleys.

TV under threat

The effectiveness of TV advertising is coming under threat. The multiplication of channels and the fragmentation of audiences is one attack. A second is the VCR fast forward button, which permits video viewers to zap the commercial breaks. Arista Technologies of Long Island have taken this function of the fast forward button a stage further. For $199, their 'Commercial Brake' black box will automatically spot and skip over any commercial recorded. It simply monitors complete breaks in sound accompanied by blank screens. According to *The Economist*, this could save the average American couch potato from sitting through 200 hours of advertisements a year.

A third assault on television is the sophistication of audiences, and their familiarity with advertising techniques. Some of the most valuable audiences also have a very low boredom threshold, expecting new ideas and concepts frequently. Combined with the trend towards shorter length commercials this means that increasingly strident and bold treatments are being deployed. Dubious tricks such as low sound levels, oblique perspectives and rapid fire action teach viewers to expect even more outlandish creativity. This may well be interpreted, with hindsight, as the end of mass media. More effective creativity is being used in narrowcast specialist channels.

Mass media are not central to Relationship Marketing. They do have a role however. In skilful hands the media can set the tone for a new brand, which can then build on this platform in more personal ways. An example is the innovative small cartoon launch adverts for the quirky Nissan Micra, which were repeated almost 'run of paper', appearing six or eight times in the same edition. These would appeal to a certain type of potential buyer and create a curiosity which could be tapped by more personal communication channels such as direct mail or telemarketing.

Business-to-business advertising

The role of advertising in business-to-business advertising is similar. Again it sets the keynote for the major activity. A fundamental tenet of Relationship Marketing is that long-term and mutually beneficial relationships are the object. Hence you will see, particularly in industrial markets, much stress is laid on the length and durability of relationships with high awareness, high status organisations.

Citibank, for example, advertised the 70 years of their continuous relationship with Caterpillar, as a means of indicating the value of their financial services to a firm with a reputation for exacting standards on its suppliers.

The audience of the advertisement goes beyond the obvious. They wish to encourage potential long-term custom to approach them or better respond to an approach by Citibank. Naturally, they are indirectly saying thank you to a major and loyal customer in a way which will possibly benefit Caterpillar's business

– the colour illustration was of an early Caterpillar model in action. Relationship Marketing is about mutuality of benefit. There are two further audiences. There are existing customers, who see that Citibank genuinely values long-term business. The message is 'stay with us, we care enough about our customers' business to support it with advertising'. The last audience is of course, the staff. With the number of employees into six figures, press advertising (and additional internal circulation) can convey values and behaviours that their employer cherishes. It is a message to think long as well as short term in relationships with customers. No bank can forget the short term, least of all when quarterly performance measures are the yardstick. However the vision must include the long term as well.

Direct response advertising

Advertising can be used very specifically to generate responses. With advertising you can cause potentially interested consumers to identify themselves to you. Mailing list creation by use of direct response advertising is a fine art of attraction and qualification.

Ford, with the launch of the Mondeo in April 1993, used 20-second television commercials to announce the launch and promote a toll-free 0800 number for prospective buyers to call for more details. Using this and parallel colour press advertising in the Sunday supplements, they generated thousands of responses. The qualifying question, 'Are you planning to change your car in the next six months?' sifted the immediate from the longer term prospects. They combined this list with the known records of Ford buyers of 12 to 36 months previously, who might now be ready to rebuy. They provided their UK dealers with 220,000

*names, including 17,000 immediate prospects. These were invit-
ed by dealers to 700 launch evenings, with a planned follow up to
those who failed to respond or respondees who did not appear at
the event.*

Rules for direct response TV advertising are exemplified by
Forte hotels. They have a memorable telephone number –
perhaps *the* most memorable number. It is 0800 40 40 40, a pun
on their own brand name. The number is centrally placed in bold
type, remains on screen for the full 8 seconds, and is twice
repeated by a voice-over.

CHECK LIST – DIRECT RESPONSE TV

- **Choose a memorable number.**

- **Display the number boldly.**

- **Visible on-screen for eight seconds.**

- **Speak the number and repeat.**

- **Urge customers to ring or record the number.**

For reasons, not fully explained, many advertising creatives
shy away from giving the response number the prominence that
it requires. This is puzzling since now 15 per cent of UK TV
advertisements have a response mechanism, and 54 per cent of
American TV adverts.

Trends in promoting fast-moving consumer goods

In fast-moving consumer goods markets, there is a move away

from television advertising. Heinz in the UK have transferred in the order of £12 million from media advertising to database building and relationship building through direct marketing. Buitoni, owned by Nestlé, are creating a European database of Italian food devotees, in support of their Pasta brand.

With press advertising and a variety of promotions Buitoni gathered around 50,000 responses to offers related to Italian food. Using a brief, but well crafted TV advertisement in limited regions, they promoted a number for consumers to ring for a new book of Italian recipes. Callers were warmly greeted by a recorded message confirming the offer and inviting them to leave their name, address and post code. Finally the recorded message thanked them for calling. The recipe book included an invitation to join the Casa Buitoni Club for lovers of Italian food, with one proof of purchase. Members receive regular newsletters, which further encourage them to enter competitions, crosswords, forward their own favourite recipes and so on. High level interaction is possible, including even visits to the actual Casa Buitoni in Tuscany. This encompasses a show kitchen and catering operation to demonstrate Italian cuisine as a centre for promotion, publicity and entertainment. This act of faith by Nestlé was accompanied by a substantial switch in the proportion of expenditure from above the line advertising to below the line promotional and direct marketing activity.

Relationship Marketing is seeing significant increases in commitment and the consequent financial and time expenditure by leading marketers.

Building relationships by direct mail

Direct mail conventionally is more flexible than media advertising, and provides the opportunity to personalise messages, by use of the recipient's name. Every opportunity carries with it a threat. The warmth engendered by the use of a personal name scores plus ten. The cold created by the incorrect or inaccurate representation of a personal name is minus twenty. If you use a name, ensure it is correct. Likewise, addresses need to be updated to reflect the movement of people. On average 7 per cent of people in Western Europe change addresses every year – skewed to the young and better off.

Direct mail has a role to play in the building and maintenance of a customer relationship, beyond its transaction-based historical routes. Its origins lie with an English gardening catalogue promoting mail order in 1667. The development came in 1886 when Richard Sears, a Northwood Minnesota railroad agent, found himself with a surplus of pocket watches to sell. He wrote to 20,000 other agents. Two years later, he was mailing a 750-page catalogue of 6,000 items all over the United States. He formed a partnership with John Roebuck and by 1902, they had a $50 million per year business.

Undoubtedly, direct mail is an effective sales medium, but in Relationship Marketing its power is greater. The ability to salute a recipient by name, and to make a personal offer, serve the need and respond further, tailoring the message and the offers to the proven likes of the individual gives it its power. This is expressed in the warmth and emotion it can sustain. Charity mailings demonstrate this ideally.

The Salvation Army – a major UK charity concerned primarily with provision of Christian support to the homeless and destitute – used direct mail to great effect with a Christmas card mailing.

Simply, existing and potential donors were sent a Christmas card to sign with a goodwill message, to be returned with a donation. The donors felt they were giving more than cash. The recipients too were receiving more than charity. According to Marketing Magazine, *response rates of 32 per cent from existing donors and 7 per cent from cold lists were achieved, with donations averaging 19 to 20. In the case of existing supporters, this was a 25 per cent increase on normal levels. Beyond this, the campaign recruited 32,000 new donors.*

This recruitment of donors demonstrates the relationship building ability of direct mail. It is the interactive aspect which creates the bond. The more interactions the more the relationship is cemented.

Two-way traffic

Interaction means response from the customer and further communication to the customer and more customer response. In effect, this is two-way traffic. To bring about this two way traffic, the company aims to make it easy for the customer to respond. Easy means providing a Freepost address, or a pre-addressed envelope or both. Charities often include a post-paid envelope, but write in the copy that sticking on a stamp saves the charity money. Many respondees affix the stamp, and that itself is a part of the interaction. The more involved they become in the process, the more involved they become with the charity.

It is not always necessary for the response to take place physically. In some cases, merely making it easy to respond should a customer so wish, builds a feeling of accessibility which supports the brand relationship. For example Persil has a bond with millions of regular purchasers.

Persil distributed a set of postcards, featuring designs in keeping with their national poster advertising. The reverse of the one of the cards describes the support available from the Persil Advisory Service – if you have any washing problems or would like to know more about the ingredients in Persil, we would be delighted to help. The number of customers sending off a completed card to Persil is certainly minuscule. However, an important point is being made to everyone seeing the cards. It says Persil are there if you need them. They are more than washing powder purveyors, they are experts on call for their customers.

Making available an advisory service boosts the bond for all customers, not simply those with washing disasters before them.

Two-way conversations

Making it easy for customers to contact you is important in commercial relationships. Easier than writing is picking up the telephone, particularly if the call is toll free, like French 'Numéros verts', or 0800 lines. Other options include local call rates wherever the call originates – better when problems of nuisance calls and line abuse arise.

Carelines are routine as a facility for most American packaged goods products. The prevalence in Europe is increasing, led by brand leaders such as Coca-Cola, Flora, Tampax, Radion, Timotei, Pillsbury bakery products, babyfoods, soups, deodorants, even Häagen-Dazs ice cream.

A survey by the L & R group in 1993, across ten product categories in various countries, showed a careline penetration of 83 per cent in the United States, 30 per cent in France, 15 per cent in Germany and 8 per cent in the United Kingdom.

What's good about carelines

Providing a careline has enormous advantages for a brand owner. It offers the message of accessibility, expertise and responsibility. If a brand is a promise of certainty, this is a way of keeping that promise. More than this the company is able to resolve misconceptions, correct errors and misunderstandings. Problems can be put right. Experience has been quoted earlier that indicates that resolved problems can result in higher loyalty from customers than for customers who have not experienced problems.

The careline can provide an agenda of issues which the company needs to address. In Japan, Kao, who make everything from face packs to floppy disks, has for some time been logging the pattern of the calls made to its product carelines. The analyses are used by the marketing department to assist with refining the communications strategy and developing new products. The callers are sufficiently interested in the product or service to ring – they are a self selecting group of high involvement purchasers. These people's views are critical. They are the often lead users or opinion leaders. When you read statistics saying that a satisfied user tells 3 friends, a dissatisfied user 13, these are the users to envisage. Convert them and they are advocates. Disenchant them and they are negative propagandists.

Record their names and phone numbers and you have a highly motivated, willing but critical test bed for new products. Industrial marketers have known this for decades. Now consumer marketers are learning from their experience.

How do you run a good careline?

The practical guidelines are available, for the cost of an aerosol can of Sunsilk hairspray, or a pack of Batchelors soup. Simply ring the careline with an ingredient question and see how they

respond. Three or four calls and you will sense the skills to emulate and the shortcomings to overcome. I offer my guidelines as a
starting point.

1 Hours of operation. They should be more than the minimum
customer expectation. The working day may be too short. 24
hours may be unnecessary. A bakery dough supplier in Italy
receives most of its calls from panic-stricken village bakers at
4 a.m. If your pack states 8 a.m. to 8 p.m., start 30 minutes
early and finish 30 minutes late.

2 Calculate how many lines you need, to be able to respond to
most callers within 30 seconds. All callers should be
answered within 3 rings, if not by an operator, then by an
answer phone with details of the likely wait time.

3 Select your staff with particular care. Interview them over the
phone and test their passion for the product. If they do not
feel committed to the brand, how can they convey enthusiasm
to callers? Radion rotate staff so that they spend no longer
than 90 minutes answering queries. It keeps their freshness of
voice. Match the voice to the brand. You expect a younger
voice on the Coke line than for Radion.

4 Train them to cover the 25 most frequently occurring issues.
Log these as they will change over time. Brief them, but do
not provide a script, let them choose the expressions with
which they feel comfortable. Role play the smooth exit from
the lonely talker, blocking the line for the next caller.

5 Give the staff exemplary back up. Specifically, they need
facts and information in accessible form, they require material to callers, a free product budget is important – if in doubt,
send it out! Back up includes linguists on call and experts. If
they do not know the answer, they must know someone who
can respond to the customer later. Finally, they must have

access to senior management if they spot a 'Big Issue' brewing.

6 Keep all promises. In fact underpromise and overdeliver, so the customer is surprised by your speed, generosity, concern.

7 Record customer names and telephone numbers, if they are willing. This builds a database of potential research subjects. You may also wish to check back on subsequent satisfaction levels. The UK is ahead of France, Germany and USA in the proportion of carelines capturing personal data.

8 Measure and monitor your effectiveness over time and against competitors.

Different industries have differing needs from a careline. Business-to-business helplines will operate differently from consumer carelines. Your market will have its unique aspects, which need to be incorporated. The final advice is to start gently and learn by doing. Avoid the fanfare launch which may set expectations rising beyond immediate capability.

Telemarketing

Just as your customers can call you, so it is possible for you to ring them. In business-to-business markets, outbound telemarketing is well established as a means of keeping in contact. It is natural for Mercury – a UK telephone company – to ring small businesses who had at some previous time expressed interest. Mercury found that less than 0.5 per cent of calls were refused. Many representatives begin the week by ringing around key customers. Routinely telesales staff will ring by arrangement for orders. Both these are valuable relationship facilitators. They convey interest, commitment and support. The essential characteristics are that the callers are known, the calls are expected and the result is helpful to the recipient.

Cold canvass calling is a different matter. It can even be a negative factor as it suggests that with no previous connection, no personal rapport, no knowledge other than public information and no introduction, the caller is seeking to make a sale. To take this point to its extremes, it is considered an insult in Guandong province of South China to make a cold call.

In Guandong, a cold call is interpreted as one of two negatives. Either the caller has no respected and willing mutual acquaintance to perform an introduction, or the effort has not been made to locate one. The message is lack of reputable connections or lack of courtesy.

Of course, cold calls can reap good results with a proficient caller, a strong proposition and a receptive listener. Nevertheless it is always preferable to have some kind of reference, introduction or support from a mutual acquaintance. With this in place, the relationship has its foundations in other successful relationships. In gardening parlance it is a graft on existing growth, not a new planting – the roots are already there.

Consumer telemarketing

For consumer markets, criticism is general about intrusive calls to homes in private time from forceful sales teams. Many Europeans act like Guandong Chinese towards the cold call. The same people fail to notice successful home-based telemarketing, when its effect is accomplished effectively. As above, if the caller is known, the call expected and the result helpful, it is not seen as 'telemarketing', but the natural effect of an existing relationship. The double-glazing hard sell is intrusive, the call from American Express to confirm safe arrival of your card is welcomed.

American Express have several objectives in their telemarketing activity. They wish to welcome new card-holders, cross-sell other services and reduce card fraud by rapid tracking of misappropriated cards. New cards are accompanied by a request for card holders to ring to verify receipt before the card was validated. Once the security checks have been carried out, the way is open for a dialogue about other services. Where new card-holders fail to call in after three weeks, outbound telemarketers call and carry out the same process. The calls are welcomed, fraud is being reduced and second year retention is rising.

A 1992 survey by the Henley Centre Planning for Social Change quizzed consumers on how happy they would be for named shops or companies to contact them by phone. The percentage who were very or fairly happy for this to take place by outlet type were as follows:

Bank where you have current account	60%
Building society with deposit account	60%
Manufacturer of your car	42%
Tour operator most recently used	42%
Shop where you do your grocery shopping	30%

In other words, where an existing relationship flourishes, telephone contact is perfectly acceptable to a large proportion of customers. Obviously overt selling is avoided, with the emphasis on checking to see that the customer is happy with the product or service. It is reasonable when satisfaction is confirmed, to follow up with information about additional relevant products or services. If the customer is pleased with existing services, more may be welcomed. Part of relationship building is sharing information and keeping associates up-to date.

Where relationships are less well established, telemarketing can fit within an integrated communication strategy. Thus the firm writes to the customer advising them of a service improvement or product enhancement, clearly stating that the letter will be followed up by a telephone call. After the call a confirmatory letter, perhaps offering a helpline number, builds further on the interactive approach.

In the best possible taste . . . a chocolate phone!

An enterprising organisation, Geneiva Chocolates of Royston, Hertfordshire, is offering a fascinating idea for use in conjunction with telephone marketing – a chocolate truffle moulded in the shape of a push button phone. Doubtless opportunities abound for its deployment in telephone-associated promotions.

Keeping customers up to date

Newsletters are another valuable way to share news and information which builds relationships. The better you know an organisation, the closer it appears to be.

Companies in rapidly changing technologies, like Microsoft and IBM, use newsletters to keep customers informed of developments. Something approaching resentment can arise in customers who are not told of updates and new releases.

IBM communicate with customers internationally with IBM Helpware. This is produced in 12 languages, has a print run of 750,000 and contains common international material, amended for local markets, and strictly local articles of interest only to the specific market.

In consumer markets, retailers have found that newsletters increase store traffic and purchasing across the range. Frequently however, these bulletins are cheaply put together. The opposite approach has been taken by Benetton.

Benetton publishes a large format full colour magazine entitled Colours. *The enterprise is, like its progenitor, truly global. With correspondents in 29 countries, 6 languages and distribution in 100 countries, it is a very high quality and expensive proposition. The objective is to convey the internationalism as it relates to the 14-to-26-year-old customer base. Thus each edition is bilingual. The journal relies more on visual images and illustrations than serious text to influence its audience.*

The Benetton style is visual with flair and emotion, the IBM approach is much more informational, and both appear to achieve objectives set for them. Readers of both would feel that the company is interested in them, their needs and curiosities.

Emotional shareholders of charities

Some charities provide newsletters or near newsletters to their regular donors and supporters. The trend in this sector is to treat supporters as emotional shareholders of the charity. Like company shareholders, they receive annual reports, quarterly information about performance and initiatives, perhaps invitations to annual meetings. Ahead of the rest, some charities are now emulating business practice in offering complete accounts or abridged versions with more illustrations and examples than figures – the donor elects which to receive.

Gifts and tokens

Gifts are exchanged to cement relationships between individuals. Likewise they work between organisations. There are dangers – the gift performs better as a thank you than as a recognition of business yet to come. Branded gifts keep the name alive on the desk or in the life of the recipient. Like the photograph on the piano, it is a reminder of the giver and their meaning to the receiver.

Branded gifts must be in keeping with the quality, image and identity of the giver.

Westland Helicopters give valued customers a little keepsake. It is a metal key ring with a releasable device enabling the user to attach and detach the ring from his belt (in this market the recipient is almost invariably male). The precision design, its smooth operation and the care of its construction supports the customer's confidence in the helicopters. If that is the care they lavish on a key ring specification, you can trust your life to the helicopter specification. The item cost is probably 50 times the price of the cheapest available key ring. The benefit is infinitely greater.

Conversely, a low quality gift can damage the credibility of the giving institution. It is a blemish on the good name. By itself it does not cause defection, but it sets off a train of thought. Seeds of doubt are sown and the customer will be primed to look for further flaws, which may culminate in the defection some time hence.

The UK has a campaigning Consumers' Association whose brand identity is 'Which?' The campaigns are directed at supporting consumer interests for good quality products and ser-

vices. They submit washing machines, cars, videos, travel ser-
vices, etc., to thorough investigations. Mercilessly they hound the
vendors of second best with the results of their elaborate and
extensive scientific product tests. To fund this activity they sell
subscriptions and books, promoted by consumer competitions
with large cash prizes. The entry forms require a signature and
to facilitate this, they have included branded Which? biros in the
envelope. The pens appear to be the cheapest available, setting
up the suspicion that they would universally fail a Which? test at
the first round!

The quality story works at PG Tips. This brand of tea has
developed a form of kitchen-based advertising partly paid for by
customers. They have on pack offers of brightly coloured tea
towels in the PG Tips livery. Customers contribute a proportion
of the cost of the tea towel. In return they receive a large, durable,
colourfast product. The quality is evident by these details. The
perception of quality is enhanced by the fact that it has been paid
for. It is not a free giveaway. PG Tips, of course, benefit from this
poster in the most relevant room of the house.

Personalisation

To the customer, their own name has a special meaning. To add
the element of personalisation is to add extra appreciation.
Guests in hotels expect headed stationery in their rooms. To find
that the headed stationery is personalised with the guest's own
name could delight. This is the experience of the Excelsior Hotel
in Hong Kong, who have found that guests mail more correspondents and hence wider awareness is built from the relationship
with the guest.

Face-to-face contact

The personal touch is greatest with personal contact, face to face. Naturally this is a vital part of Relationship Marketing. Since it is not possible on many occasions, it has to be managed superlatively well when it does occur. The customer will build up a picture of the company from purchases, advertising, direct mail and telephone contact. It is vital that the goodwill created is not dissipated by the personal contact. It must live up to expectation. As with the weekend together of the imaginary couple working in different areas, the critical moments are the first and last minutes. To encapsulate the strength of the relationship the greeting and farewell must be highspots. An untoward expression or word at either time can have long term remorse, or annoyance. This is important in commercial transactions too.

A major retailer has a deliberate policy of locating the most experienced, enthusiastic and positive shop assistants close to the front of the store. The newer and less convincing staff are found tills further away from the entrance. Thus the first and last impressions of the retail customer are most likely to be positive.

Other organisations manage it slightly differently. A leading bank in Seattle has meeters and greeters. As account holders enter the premises they are welcomed and directed to the appropriate service. The expression 'Missing you already' is probably an abuse of the farewell element. It is executed far more effectively in an English pub.

Industrial salesmen are taught that you have 90 seconds to make a positive impression, and that the last minute can undo all the good work done.

Encouraging face to face contact

For many organisations, it is helpful to increase the amount of face-to-face contact. The UK retailer Habitat, part of the IKEA group, found an effective way of achieving this.

Habitat sell through retail stores and also with a catalogue. This is extensive and attractive and is sold for £2. Regular buyers are naturally provided with a free copy of the catalogue. The practice had been to mail the customers with free copies of their catalogue. The new initiative was simply to write to the customers announcing the new catalogue, including an invitation to visit the store and collect their free copy there. This has boosted the relationship because everyone likes an invitation and the warm welcome when they arrive. It has also markedly enhanced sales. Customers see and buy the merchandise.

In business-to-business marketing, it can be helpful to invite customers to your premises more often than your rivals do. Even service companies can create evening events in their offices which are appreciated by those who turn up and also by those who received invitations but declined them.

'It only seems like yesterday'

Creating events leads naturally to celebrating anniversaries. This is a way in which couples recognise and enjoy their relationship. So too it can be applied to commercial relationships. Take the buyer out to dinner to celebrate 20 years business together. Send congratulations telegrams and a model digger to the dealer sales force when they sell their 100th JCB backhoe loader. Give the customer a free ticket to next month's performance when he or she arrives at their 100th show. The memory of a surprise (or short notice) celebration can last a lifetime. It is the unexpected pleasure which adds sparkle to a commercial and personal relationship.

Your top customers

Entertainment is a valuable way of getting close to your most frequent users and customers. You can show your appreciation of their business, and in the relaxed atmosphere unpressured by business routines, you may gain feedback to take your business forward.

Swissair studied their customer flight records and discovered just how important to them were their top 50 fliers. The senior management took groups of these customers (plus partners), away for weekends. The events were very successful for both airline and customers.

The entertainment as a genuine appreciation for past business helps nurture the relationship and also gives the host the opportunity to listen learn and consider ways of bettering service.

Entertaining millions of customers?

Event sponsorship is a way in which companies can entertain millions of customers at a time. Multi-nationally, it represents a way forward when there are few global TV advertising opportunities. We see Sony, McDonalds, Marlboro, Coca-Cola all attaching their names to world class sponsorships in football, the Olympics, motor racing and other sporting attractions. The benefit is that it places the brand in the spotlight and acts as a prompt and reminder. The event must naturally meet criteria of suitability for the brand and its values, and interest levels to consumers. This is mass marketing, not Relationship Marketing. Going beyond the event itself and surrounding it with relationship building activity is the touch of the professional. Dollar for dollar matching is the budget for success. For every dollar spent on the event, add another for merchandising, promotions, hospitality, competitions and prizes.

Carling Black Label is a Canadian lager brand, now the largest UK beer brand under the management of the licensed brewer Bass. For a sum of £12 million over four years, Carling is sponsoring the Football Association Premier League. The 1993/4 season delivered the mass marketing benefits of 10,000,000 attendances at matches plus countless mentions in the sports columns of thousands of newspapers. To bring the sponsorship into the lives of lager drinkers, Bass installed merchandise kits in 10,000 bars and pubs. They subsidised the installation of satellite dishes in hundreds of pubs with encouragement to drinkers to watch Monday night televised matches there. Promotions were run with local radio stations and local press to reward Carling drinkers with prizes of entertainment at football matches. Finally, they linked the sponsorship to the product itself by producing special cans commemorating their involvement. The sponsorship has come out of the football stadium, into the bar and further right into the hand of the armchair drinker. Relationships work: at a time of lager market decline, sales rose 10 per cent over the equivalent period before the sponsorship.

So with creativity and determination, Carling Black Label developed their relationship with their millions of drinkers.

The BIG opportunity you can never foresee

Getting to know customers, delivering products which satisfy with reliability, communicating with them frequently with phone calls, helplines, newsletters, entertainment and business gifts all develop relationships. They do this in a smooth and progressive manner. On a graph of warmth and mutual esteem, the line would start slowly and curve upwards with increasing understanding and business proximity. There is something which is able to take that line suddenly up to a new level. On a computer generated graph, there would be a line break while the computer recalibrated the x axis.

What is this something?

Let us return to the image of a couple, working apart. One breaks a leg. The other joins them immediately. No priority comes before this. It is being there in a crisis.

Being there in a crisis

In a business context, a computer crashes without a back up. The major product supplier immediately calls in staff over the weekend to create new records from the supply details and furnishes them on Sunday night to the home of the desperate customer. A warehouse burns down and the manufacturer lends stock, fork lifts and people to keep the firm in business. In a personal situation, the bank takes the widow carefully through all the essential financial transactions and decisions previously handled by the partner. Whatever happens thereafter, no-one can prise the customer from the supplier who was there in the moment of crisis. Yes, the supplier could ultimately drive the customer away with abominable service, but other than this the bond is forever. There is no offer a competitor can make to overturn the loyalty engendered by this act.

Not being there!

The opposite thought does not need a great deal of developing. Suppose the manufacturer foreclosed on the poor wholesaler and brought him to bankruptcy . . .

Be ready when it happens

Since you have no idea when a customer may strike misfortune needing your support, readiness is the only precept. The priority is to make staff aware of the posture you wish to adopt – as it is they who will encounter the problem first and be responding perhaps even before the senior management are aware. Initiative is fostered by legend. When the smallest of deeds in this area surfaces, celebrate, recognise and congratulate the individual concerned. Talk incessantly about the value of this initiative. Create a company legend. Soon the second issue will arise and a like performance will begin to set a pattern. The action is not quite without reference to costs. That way lies your own bankruptcy. But cost is a minor consideration at the hour of disaster. In fact, in most instances the financial impact on a major corporation is minute and less than the invoice for a piece of lavish entertainment. Which would the desperate wholesaler prefer?

Integration

The chapter began with stressing the concept of consistency of communication across all channels. With the variety of means at the firm's disposal, integration is an essential task. Manuals are out of date before they are printed. The only formula I know is precedent. It evolves as circumstances change. Familiar approaches proceed without hindrance. New messages need to be approved.

SUMMARY

- Communication is the essence of relationship building. It is built upon the foundations of first-class staff, the right customers for you and the excellence and appropriateness of the product or service. Communication pulls it all together and acts as the cement.

- The guidelines to communication effectiveness include: frequency, consistency, correct tone of voice, interaction between customer and supplier, and as much personalisation as possible.

- All methods of communication need to work effectively and in harmony with each other, and in harmony with the customer so that a complete dialogue occurs. The more contact, often the greater the relationship. Of all the features of communication, the most important is the least predictable: being there in a crisis, the message that I am here by your side is a fundamental piece of communication which is never forgotten.

10

WORD-OF-MOUTH MARKETING

Marketing communications are initiated by the organisation to convey the uses and benefits of the product or service. They are intentionally interactive so that feedback aids organisational learning. This interactive approach leads to relationships being built as an organisational strategy. These strategies work directly and the communications elements have been covered in the previous chapter. There is another communications strategy working indirectly. This chapter covers the part of communications known as word-of-mouth marketing.

Word-of-mouth marketing occurs naturally with well-produced products, which are discussed positively by consumers with potential consumers. Users make recommendations to others and a swell of popular opinion progressively endorses the service. Favourable momentum supports the brand in its consumer acceptance. The value is immense, because of its impartiality and its credibility. There is one drawback. Word-of-mouth marketing tends to work very slowly.

Speeding up the process

It is possible to increase the effectiveness of word-of-mouth marketing and this is an important strand in the overall Relationship Marketing strategy. To bring this about requires the platform of first class products, services and customer satisfaction, to which are added specific techniques. These are described in a sequence. This acts as a résumé of some of the ideas which have been covered elsewhere.

The objective is to encourage more people to recommend your brand, more often to more potential customers.

1 What does 'better' mean?

The learning organisation will have a clear understanding of the perceived relative quality compared with rival brands. Beyond this, research must be distilled to uncover the aspects which drive those perceptions. How do customers assess and judge that quality? How does the user demonstrate the product superiority to a friend? For a chainsaw, it is noise related. For a car, the car door slam mystically conveys excellence. For a portable tape player, it is the smoothness of the closing mechanism. For a mattress, it is the finger depression test 30 centimetres from the edge. Observe how customers show off their model and ensure the specification works to their advantage.

Listen to users talking. How do they describe the betterness? What phrases do they employ? This can give clues to the direction product development needs to focus upon. This may also suggest benefit statements for brochures, advertisements and mailings. Finally, what don't they say about your product? There may be clues here about relative shortcomings. Knowing what 'better' means in the actions and words of the proud users is a valuable insight.

2 How is the product or service delivered?

The next stage is to observe the human element in the delivery of the product or service. What comments are made about this by users. Listen beyond the relevant comments. What irrational and emotional prejudices influence the perception of the service?

How the driver is dressed may have no impact on the style of his driving, his courtesy on the road, or the timeliness of his deliveries, but if the customer has a better perception of better dressed delivery crews, that is a service reality. It works because it stimulates conversations. On-time delivery is not a conversation starter – late delivery of course is! However, if you have that delivery standard AND your drivers are well turned out, it is the appearance that will create the positive endorsement by the customer to a potential user.

The Carlisle-based UK haulage company, Eddie Stobart, run 450 immaculate red and green lorries. The company insists their drivers wear ties and drive with courtesy at all times. They receive up to 50 letters per day from people complimenting them on the good driving of their employees. A fan club, set up in 1990, now has 7,000 members.

3 What do customers complain about?

Take serious note of your complainers. As said before, they are interested enough in your product to comment and complain. Most users simply walk away, quietly choosing not to buy again. People who complain are valuable. Rectifying the problem is stage one. Resolved problems create greater loyalty than an absence of problems. Most travellers expect the airline to lose their luggage, and stand worrying at the reclaim carousel. Those of us who have actually had luggage in Bangkok, when we are in Heathrow, know how well we are looked after, and have a far higher satisfaction rating. Complaints are an opportunity.

Turning the complainant into an advocate is stage two. Over-compensation is not the answer. Fair compensation, followed by continuing interest pays higher dividends. Call them again, a month later to check that they are now completely happy. Do they have any other comments or suggestions? Should you ever implement an idea from one of these individuals, write and let them know beforehand to give them the chance to tell their friends. Complainers are unconverted advocates, who identify themselves to you. Complainers are an opportunity.

4 How to get recommendations – simply try asking.

Many satisfied customers would willingly suggest potential clients or customers and allow you to use their name in recommendation. A courteous approach which places them under no obligation is usually all that is required. Good manners dictate that recommendations should be used diplomatically, quickly and without any exaggeration. Marginal under-statement on your part, if followed by enthusiastic support from your recommender, is the ideal pattern.

5 Advertising can help.

Your advertising may well be read avidly by your existing users and ignored by the type of loyal customer you would like to attract from a competitor. Write your advertisement as a script for the users, so that they can present the arguments personally to customers you cannot reach. Some observers believe that this is an objective of the Volvo advertising strategy.

Truly creative advertising can be used to stimulate conversation in their own right. Two examples convey this, one Dutch and the other 'double Dutch'. The first example is the legendary brilliance of Apeldoorn – the leading Dutch insurance company. TV commercials depict hilarious disasters, each more dramatic than the last, and all ending with the line – just call Apeldoorn. The reputation is so great that advertising creative teams find themselves bombarded with even more creative ideas from other staff and viewers. Their crowning glory is the poster advert poached from the glue advertiser. They stuck a Trabant on the side of a large roadside hoarding, purporting to be the glue advert. Three days later the Trabant lay dented on the ground, the hoarding had a huge hole in it, underneath which was the slogan just call for Apeldoorn. That created conversation!

The second example is double Dutch, in other words, fake Dutch. In order to stimulate conversation, Carlsberg-Tetley, who sell the Dutch lager Oranjeboom in the UK, ran a poster and bus side campaign which at first sight appeared to be in Dutch. Careful reading of the words produced phonetically a typically English phrase. To assist drinkers with the more obscure slogans, a customer help line was installed. Another conversation creator!

6 The celebrity endorsement.

Consumers fall into various bands of willingness to experiment, according to Everett M. Rogers. Progressing from the innovators, through early adopters, the early majority, the late majority, the sequence finishes with the laggards. Innovators need no endorsement, and early adopters follow the innovators. Informative advertising and recommendation appeals to the early majority. For the cautious late majority and the ultra conservative laggards, solid reassurance is necessary. Celebrity backing can provide much of this. Celebrities have the advantage that fans like to talk about them, and this can stimulate word-of-mouth comment. The risk is always that the star will overshadow the product. This is truer for stars who are multi-product advertisers, so these renta-celebs are to be avoided. Mega-stars can also fall from favour. As with a sponsorship, carry the endorsement into promotions, point of sale material, newsletters and so on. The link between Nike and Michael Jordan is a successful example.

7 Event sponsorship.

The Carling Black Label branding of the FA Premier League is an example, already mentioned, of a sponsorship fully exploited and merchandised which prompted word-of-mouth advertising. Drinkers could hardly fail to mention the connection.

8 Sampling to the opinion leaders.

If you want opinion leaders to recommend your product or service they must have first hand experience. Provide samples of Bacardi to the bright young things in Bangkok if your aim is to build the brand in Thailand. Apple built its brand partly through providing sample computers to the universities of Silicon Valley, California, where graduating students demand the latest in equipment when they start work. Who influences your users, and do they have direct personal knowledge of the product? If they are happy with your product they will recommend it, and more importantly, potential buyers will listen.

9 Let your product be seen in the right places.

A brand is judged by the company it keeps. In some categories, the brand is who wears it. Define the environment you wish to be seen in and seek it out. Sony are acknowledged professionals in this arena. Their brands placed in James Bond films provoked comment and emulation. To establish the Sony Walkman, the company paid beautiful young people to parade around Ginza Park at weekends, listening to their Walkman models. They were noticed which led to talk. Talk led to action, and sales took off.

10 Advertise your long-term customers.

Fill your advertisements with examples of long time satisfied customers, quote them, place their products boldly in your advertising to benefit their awareness. Show photographs of your customers in your brochures, list your clients. Eurocamp, the fixed site camping holiday company, promote their sites with photographs supplied by their customers. There are many reasons for this technique. Firstly, your client will be delighted and increase the promotion and endorsement on a personal level. Secondly, you have a halo effect of the brand with which you are linking, and that link is more noticeable than an advert with only one brand in it. Finally, it will strike a chord with other users in conversation with a dissatisfied customer of a rival. Your customer can offer his or her own experience and back it up with the example in the advert to create a double impact.

11 Public relations.

The editorial of a newspaper is much more readily believed than the paid advertising. The route to the editorial is through public relations. A creative idea can run and run. All credit to the wine growers of Beaujolais for their connection of a date and a wine, to create a race with the year's new bottling. The opportunity for stimulating conversation about your brand in the media is immense. Creativity applied here can be more valuable than in advertisement design. The authority that the annual *Lex Report on Motoring* has provided to the car distribution and leasing firm could not have been developed through advertising.

12 Come to our seminar.

An invitation is always worthy of a mention. Holding relevant and topical seminars by invitation only can result in clamour for places. Offering close customers the chance to invite colleagues from other businesses will have them on the phone to people spreading word of your expertise.

13 Run a promotion, catch a recommendation.

The standard promotional techniques are aimed at winning business directly. Good word-of-mouth promotions capture business indirectly. The aim is to use your customers to promote your business and gain in so doing. The break up of the telephone monopolies has led to intense competition, not least in the United States of America. By signing up with Sprint, a customer received a 20 per cent discount on the three numbers called most frequently, or 36 per cent discount if the number happened to be another Sprint subscriber – an excellent way to encourage word-of-phone recommendation.

14 Give the team the story and they'll sell for you.

Your staff, their families, the staff in your suppliers and distributors and their families have an interest in your success. They ought to be predisposed to recommend your product or service to everyone they encounter. Phase one is to encourage them to do so. This can be as simple as asking them to do this. You can make it easy for them with hot lines, contact names, information on clues to look for in seeking potential clients. Phase two is to provide them with the positive case so that they can sell the benfits in their own words. Let them become sales staff by making the corporate staff communication video less of a diatribe and more of a sales training session with lots of concrete examples. Show them the way it is done in practice. Share this video with your suppliers and their staff. If every member of your support team (employed by you or not) knew the order winning benefits well enough to mention them in a bar or over a meal, with ease and conviction, the results could be immense. When Fosters' Draught was launched on to the UK lager market in 1983, much of its wildfire success could be attributed to the selling activity of drivers, technicians, accountants, foremen, secretaries, cleaners as well as the professional sales staff. The total company was briefed on the launch and how to sell it.

SUMMARY

- Word-of-mouth support for your brand will only spring up if you deserve it. Then it will flow naturally, but at a trickle. To boost this to a full flood requires a sensitive prompting of existing customers to allow you to use their names, and to promote you themselves. Advertising, promotions, product placement and sponsorships can all be used to good effect. The largest opportunity, however, may well be closest to home with the stakeholders of your own firm.

- Plan to deploy word-of-mouth marketing as part of the Relationship Marketing communications strategy.

11

TRAINING FOR SERVICE EXCELLENCE

Relationship Marketing relies heavily on the people in your organisation who personify the relationship for the customers and clients. In Chapter 5 we considered the recruitment of the right staff to form the loyal base an organisation requires. We also looked at the ways to retain and motivate them. This is the springboard for elevating them to the levels of excellence your customers deserve. This chapter looks at the training which creates this excellence.

For many businesses, sustaining a unique selling advantage with their products is challenging. The pace of technology and the pressure of industry standards is driving many markets to offer undifferentiated products. It is often relatively straightforward for competitors to replicate a new product, sometimes in very short-time frames. Some Japanese food companies have eschewed test marketing, when they fear being beaten to the full-scale launch by fleet-footed competitors matching their innovation. In these markets, service is the only differentiator. What you offer is very similar to competitors. How you offer it is substantially better.

Beefeater are the leading licensed restaurant chain in the United Kingdom. Their lead is less about the menus they provide – though these are up-to-the-minute, reflecting increasingly international tastes – less about the facilities, and much more about the service culture of the staff. Beefeater succeed with a number of life stage target segments. One segment, for example, is the retired, who typically dislike inconsistency and surprise in their eating out. For them Beefeater have established an Emerald Club, whose membership now stands at 220,000. To succeed with this segment is a testimony to the training which maintains consistently high standards in over 300 outlets. More than 9,000 staff have exceeded the 90 per cent standard in the Beefeater Service Excellence Programme. Beefeater gained a National Training Award for this achievement.

The differential advantage that competitors find it so hard to replicate is this service consistency. Menus and facilities can be copied without difficulty, but a trained staff with a culture of service cannot be imitated so readily.

And all companies are service companies. Somewhere someone is providing a service.

Agreed, but where do you start?

The right staff is the starting point. Without potential, no amount of dedicated training and development can succeed. Having followed the earlier guidelines, and selected ideal candidates, the deployment of staff is the priority. Some talented, willing, well motivated people prefer to act as support to their forward facing colleagues. Others enjoy the pleasure and hassles of face to face contact with customers.

This is the division between two types of staff. In his book, *Frontiers of Excellence* 1994 (published in the USA as 'What America Does Right'), Robert Waterman cites the example of Federal Express. He describes the care that they take to match staff to front or back office roles. It is legitimate to elect for the relative normality of supporting internal colleagues. It is equally right for others to choose the outward facing position. The problems arise when the square peg is forced into the round hole. Are staff matched to their talents and orientation?

What do you expect of me?

Setting clear standards for employees and communicating them effectively is the basis for their understanding of the organisation's objectives. This means two things. Firstly, it helps staff set their own standards. Secondly, it involves staff member and manager in the gap analysis that specifies training needs.

Setting out the goals of the organisation normally results in a mission statement. Mission statements tend to be indigestible, polysyllabic aspirations encompassing every conceivable virtue. Multi-objective statements blur into meaninglessness. They must spell out what action is needed and be a call to taking that action. There are two tests. The first is for comprehension. Could an intelligent nine year old understand every word and the meaning of the statement? Secondly, would it be sufficient policy guidance if a customer crisis arose on the night shift?

The examples of unsuccessful mission statements are legion. There are fewer models to emulate. The most impressive on both the above criteria is the Automobile Association, whose activities range from roadside rescue to publishing motoring and related books, including 220 retail outlets and an insurance arm. To link these disparate operations into a common standard of service the AA have a focused mission statement. It takes the form of a speech bubble, below which is the statement, 'When every member and customer can say this, we will be irresistible.' The speech bubble reads:

> I instinctively turn to the AA – you are always there, easy to reach
> and ready to help. You have standards I can trust and you impress
> me more every time you serve me and solve my problems.

This gives a clear steer to the direction any employee should
move in serving customers and solving their problems. Master-
care, a subsidiary of Firestone in the servicing part of the American automotive industry, express a similar thought in different
words. Their stated goal is to give customers an 'experience that
will encourage them to return willingly and to share their
experience with others'.

Setting standards is not easy

Beyond the mission statement, most service organisations measure their performance. The danger is that what is measured tends
to be the easy not the important. Favourite of all standards
appears to be the answering of the phone within three rings. This
is very straightforward to measure, and analysis can demonstrate
the percentage success achieved. Without implying that speed is
not important, I should like to suggest that the outcome of the call
is more significant than the initial response time. Checking the
satisfaction with service using a balanced survey of representative customers tracked over time published in the form of a satisfaction index is a better measure. The objective is to have a happy
customer, not a mechanical telephone operation consistently
answering after 4.5 seconds.

Let the teams develop the guidelines

The measurement is the customer satisfaction index, but guidelines are still useful as an aid to staff. They know the critical

nature of the index, and will have their own ideas on how to influence it. As an idea, why not allow an element of self management in the team. With the index as the target, teams can develop their own guidelines, with management available for consultation if requested. Reviewed and updated over time, these self generated guidelines invariably raise standards. They work for two reasons. Contact staff know better what influences customers. Staff who make their own rules are more committed to them – they have ownership and control.

Owning your development plan

The same ownership is important for development plans. The needs are based on assessment of current knowledge, skills and behaviours, compared with the desired levels. The gap is the development plan. Through the mission statement and the expected standards, linked to the knowledge of market and industry changes, there will ideally be a joint acceptance of the training objectives. Self assessment of needs is followed by confirmation of those needs and collaboration on the best options to meet them.

A personal development log

For implementation, the suggestion is to equip every member of staff with their own personal training log at the outset. They hold the log and they record in it all their training and development experiences. This includes skills training, internal and external programmes and seminars attended, internal presentations, personal learning, specific reading, observing others, inter-functional experience and time with sales teams and customers. The log must reflect active learning. The log is the core of regular manager subordinate reviews. Its message is that training is a joint responsibility, not a matter of management dosage at regular intervals.

Individual responsibility goes further

The individual responsibility can extend to briefing sessions of work groups by any-one who has encountered and handled a new situation. Encouraging the sharing of experience is the dynamic of the learning organisation. Management cannot know all the questions let alone all the answers. The success of the enterprise is a collective commitment.

Training goes further

You train your own staff, of course. You may train your customers' staff in the usage of your product or the best retailing techniques to employ. Do you train your suppliers' staff in how best to meet your needs? Do you train the temporary or contract staff who serve your customers? The wave of contracting out of services and functions has led in many instances to your customers being served by contractors. Who now makes your deliveries for you? Do you train those drivers in courtesy, tact, helpfulness, product handling characteristics . . .

Training bring warmth and confidence

Training has its own intrinsic merits in the way it can boost operational efficiency and competence. There is also a warmth and confidence that it imparts. The warmth comes from the feeling that for the organisation to be investing in me, I must be valued. The confidence comes from the sense of being prepared for whatever comes my way.

Who really trains the staff?

The concept of training that sits in the front of the mind probably derives from school days, with an image of desks, paper and an expert teacher. Company learning is not like this. It is a collection of personal assessments of new knowledge, observations of others in practice, tests and experiments, reviews and consolidations of new experiences into practice. It is an active process. The workplace is the classroom. The tools of the trade, like the till, the telephone, the computer replace the paper. There is no expert teacher, instead there are role models, good, bad, realistic and unrealistic. Who really trains your staff? Partly the role models and partly they are self-taught through experience.

What does this mean?

The consequence of this is that if you wish to run a successful operation of any type you need to know who are the key influences on your staff. In any group of people, natural leaders will emerge. Within 24 hours, someone will normally become accepted in this role. It is not age based, though seniority is significant, particularly in South-east Asia. It is not education or status driven, nor do physical attributes define it. Somehow one voice is more listened to than others. It is observable in the school playground, in a project team, in a canteen bridge group. In a work team, they may be the supervisor, but not necessarily. You need to know who acts in this role, as they are the role models. Standards cannot be imposed as successfully as they can be implemented by these people. Observation, conversation and body language of deference can identify them, if you do not already know them. Armed with this knowledge, you can respect their positions and influence them to support the behaviours you aim to inculcate. Their influence is hopefully benign. If they are positive and promotable, they make the best supervisors and managers. On occasions, the powerful influence in the work group is a negative factor. This is an instance where you must act to remove them. Their hostility to change, to the direction the company is taking, or simply to the customer ethic, inhibits the success potential.

Do as I do (not do as I say)

Managers, directors and the chief executive officers are also organisational role models. The lesson here is that staff are deaf to the words, but hear the actions. They imitate the behaviour far more than they respond to exhortations. What does the managing director place first on his agenda? No amount of words will convince staff that the company is market driven or focused on innovation for customers, if the meeting spends the first one-and-a-half hours on financial statements before the market issues are reached. Live your priorities, allocate your time, energy and communication accordingly.

Legends and stories

Children learn much of their understanding of life, good and evil, success and failure from legends and fairy stories. Actually so do company employees, but we do not call them fairy stories! The book *Management by Legends* is yet to be written, but the power of company anecdotes and mythology is great. Rather than a policy manual on the careful use of the brand logo, the legend circulates of a former managing director who threw a whole consignment of brochures from a sixth floor window when the logo was incorrect. Federal Express have stories of gallant delivery crews delivering the package through hurricanes.

Land-Rover staff tell of the security man on duty during the Christmas close down, who extracted a vital component from the stores and dispatched it to the Defender driver stranded in Croatia, providing telephone instructions on how to fit it.

Stories and legends spell out the culture in a colourful and memorable fashion. With frequent repetition, they command a respect and influence behaviour far more than any instruction could achieve. Clearly, Land-Rover have built a relationship for ever with one Defender driver in particular, and shown the example to every other employee. The employees have a role model.

Messages, subtle and not so subtle

The messages management wish to communicate are best sent with subtlety. There is one American company that prints on its employees' salary envelopes: 'Brought to you by the customer'. The message is clear, but perhaps heavy-handed. Maybe a more subtle approach could achieve the desired result. Legends are often stronger than the printed word.

Training about 'now'

Part of training is to refresh and update staff. To keep them informed of new initiatives and changes is to keep them thinking afresh. 'What is new?' is the first question when a staff member returns from a holiday. Why only then? Create the sense of something new every week. Staff communication and training come close together. Any communication will include a part that influences behaviours, directly or indirectly.

Sainsbury is a major UK grocery retailer. The advertising devised for them by their agency, Abbot Mead Vickers SMS, presented their slogan, 'Good food costs less at Sainsbury's' in a particularly visual way. The TV advert took the form of close-up photographic depiction of a recipe for an excellent platter, using Sainsbury's branded ingredients, whose total cost was eminently affordable. Two weeks before the advert was screened, every employee, part time, full time, in every location, had the chance to see it. One week beforehand, the dish appeared on the canteen menus to allow staff to try it. Staff also received the menu cards before they were displayed in store to test the recipe themselves.

All staff were informed. All staff felt involved. Any shelf stacker would recognise a customer request for directions to the aisle where the essential ingredient was shelved. They would be able to answer for sure, but they would answer with an air of confidence. They knew why the customer was asking. They were on the inside. They had seen the advert, understood its significance, and now had the opportunity to finalise the process.

Thus communication has a training ingredient in boosting confidence in customer contact. Naturally, the sales results of the particular ingredients were communicated to employees.

Instant impressions

The customer meeting the confident and enthusiastic shelf stacker gained an instant and positive impression. This first contact experience is a vital part of Relationship Marketing. The confidence and expertise sets the buyer at ease. It says, you are in safe hands.

There are two parts to this impression. One is the appearance, demeanour and air of confidence. This contributes significantly, and a poor visual impression may curtail the contact at that point. An acceptable or positive visual set of clues takes the customer to the second part. This is the impression given by the words that are spoken. In telephone contact, the words are all. In fact that is where most of the research on impressions has been undertaken.

Simple techniques are readily taught. They are not tricks to outwit customers. In a relationship that type of behaviour is out of order. Rather they are pointers to make the contact easier to understand, evaluate and respond.

How do you give your name to a customer?

Names are important. Knowing the name of the person you are speaking to establishes a rapport. There are dozens of word combinations to give your name to a customer. Most result in the customer knowing they have been given the name, but not being able to register it. In this instance, giving the name is actually counterproductive. Research tends to suggest that the best format, especially over the phone, is to say, 'Good afternoon, my name is Tony Cram'. The wording informs the customer that a name is coming before it is actually stated. Facts that you want remembered are best placed at the end of a sentence where they have prominence.

Before the name is given, there should be a statement of the company, department, division or service represented. Familiar scripts trip off the tongue easily. Repetition increases the familiarity, and often the delivery speed of the phrase is very rapid. The pressure on rapid answering spills over into the introduction. To the caller, the phrase is unfamiliar and they are tuning in to the new voice or accent. Rehearsing a normal pace of delivery is helpful to customers, who are then sure they are speaking to the right department, know the name and understand you are ready to help.

Don't let the customer realize it's your fiftieth call today

The magic ingredient in relationships is enthusiasm. The fiftieth customer should feel as if they were the first. The first call of the day bounce carried through makes customers respond positively. More than any other factor, this distinguishes the warm bond from the duty call. If customers sense that the person on the end of the phone line, or standing in front of them is enthusiastic, the rapport is already beginning to form. Keeping up enthusiasm is a challenge, when you spend a day taking customer calls. Yet it makes the difference.

Present the problem to the retail staff and the telephonists and account handlers. Let them draw conclusions about the ways to deliver the same freshness to every customer. Let them test competitors and develop strategies for their own style. They can discuss break times, the need for time out after the hassle call, mutual feedback. The results will be significant.

Lasting impressions

There are two critical moments in a customer contact. The first greeting to establish rapport, competence and willingness to help creates an impression. The final phrases leave the lasting impression. Relationship Marketing suggests that the lasting impression is the one that influences whether the customer returns.

What makes a good close to a book, movie or play?

If the close has so much significance, what are the secrets of success? Using the parallel of a book or a play is relevant. Every time a Disney employee is visible to customers, they describe it as being on stage. When you are with customers you are giving a performance. If it is good they will return for more. There are four secrets to a successful close.

1 **There are no loose ends.** When the play finishes, you know what has happened to each of the central characters. Unlike a soap opera, there is no cliff hanger to grip your intention until the next instalment.

  The customer contact should conclude with no loose ends. This has two parts, the real and the perceived. The account handler must endeavour to cover all the issues raised and also confirm that this is the case. To give the perception of completeness, the question should be put: Has that covered everything? Ensure that the customer comes back with a positive confirmation.

2 **The ending meets the expectations set up at the beginning.** The book has maintained its interest to the end. The actors do not appear eager to get off the stage.

  The customer should never feel that their time is up and the account handler is impatient to take the next call, or next person in line. The warmth of the greeting must be reinforced at the close. Business completed, there should be an enthusiastic thank you for calling, or coming in.

3 **The play feels as if it was written just for you.** The book strikes a chord with your feelings, experiences or attitudes. You want to write your name in the front.

  The customer should feel that this is a unique call or meeting, personal to them. Personalise the last part of the call. The use of the customer's name should be mandatory, when the conversation is closing.

4 **A good book stimulates you to look for the sequel, or other works by the same author, or in the series.** You seek out other films featuring the star of the movie.

In some way, probably indirectly, act in a way that will encourage them to come back for more.

Training and development are therefore, preparation for the performance. Some staff are front of house, others are back stage. Both have an indispensable role to play. Neither would survive without the other.

Training is a secret

Organisations which invest heavily in training feel justly proud of their efforts. There is a spotlight on training and it rises up the scale of corporate interest. When it reaches a certain point, a temptation tantalises. It goes like this. Everyone agrees that training is a good thing. We do a lot of training. Why don't we announce how much training we do in our advertisements. Customers will believe we are a good company to do business with. Sadly, it does not work so simply. Training is a secret. The results are visible and appear to be natural.

Never boast of your training, let customers discover and appreciate it for themselves. Likewise never boast of your service standards – it invites criticism in the moments you cannot deliver. In addition, it sets up unrealistic expectations:

> I am going to tell you a really funny joke, probably the best one you have ever heard. It will leave you rolling in the aisles. It is sensational, so new, so clever . . .

No joke can live up to that build-up. Promoting the wonders of your service is best left to your loyal and positive customers. Let them promote you through word-of-mouth advertising. In another chapter there are suggestions to facilitate this.

SUMMARY

- In a world where making a different product is increasingly hard, there is a way of standing out from the competitors. It is through service – the hardest part of the mix to copy.

- Service excellence depends on the right staff and the support systems. It also depends on training. Training is a joint responsibility between staff member and manager. More than training courses, it means learning from experience, experiment and example. Role models are critical. Management should act as models themselves. They should also monitor departmental role models and support this with company legends.

- Service techniques can be taught to aid customers. The reality must include the magic ingredient, enthusiasm. Together with personalisation, the relationship can be developed in those moments of customer contact. They make the difference.

12

BRINGING IT ALL TOGETHER

A successful company is a directed web of relationships, anticipating and responding to customer needs, and thereby delivering sustainable returns to its shareholders. A successful enterprise in the voluntary or public sector is similarly a web of relationships, meeting the needs of users and beneficiaries to the satisfaction of the trustees. Leading the organisation to function as such a web of internal relationships is the task of management. This chapter addresses the challenge for management of bringing the ideas together in an applicable form. It summarises the priorities when an organisation wishes to implement Relationship Marketing.

Four questions for the chief executive

There are four stages which can be encapsulated in four questions for the chief executive to answer. Diagrammatically they can be portrayed as a square, since they lead from one to the next, and the final question returns to the first.

1 Where is the organisation going? The strategy.
2 How does it get there? The business plan.
3 Is it learning as it goes? Operational application.
4 Is it getting there? The results.

Return to Question One.

The chief executive is not solely responsible for answering these questions, but to create the web of relationships which is capable of answering them. Management in the 1990s is inspirational collaboration – the chief executive provides the inspiration and ensures the collaboration takes place.

Where is the organisation going?

The fundamental responsibility of the chief executive is to have a vision of the current position of the organisation and where it will be in the future. With all the difficulties of prediction this is an unfolding vision, modified by the continuing experiences within its context of political, economic, social, technological and competitive forces.

This responsibility has three phases:

- Identifying the shape of the market.

- Isolating the strategy.

- Implementing.

To set the direction for an ocean liner, maritime charts are required. To set the direction for an organisation, the charts are the patterns of the interplaying factors which go to make a market more or less attractive for that organisation. The calibration of the growth, health, profitability, durability and security of markets leads to one scale of attractiveness of a given market. The assessment of the skills, talents, resources and unique capabilities of the organisation provides a second scale.

Combining the two scales points to the markets which the organisation feels itself ideally suited to attack, defend or abandon.

The markets to abandon are those where no differential advantage can be defined and communicated. In these commodity markets, the lowest price rules and profits are under permanent pressure.

Isolating the strategy

The strategy, where an advantage can be obtained, must be defence in existing markets and attack in potential markets. The differential advantage offered by Relationship Marketing is the power of loyalty. Are there, or could there be a sufficiently large body of customers who respond, or would respond to your offering with a loyal purchasing pattern? Does the firm have the talents, skills and resources to provide an offering which would be sufficiently attractive to earn and retain their loyalty. These two perspectives identify the markets the Relationship Marketing based organisation should focus upon.

Strategic focus

The platform is the core of loyal users. Typically, in mature markets, growth comes from increasing their usage and patronage, as described in Chapter 3, and also from the new business gained from similar customers recruited by referral and word-of-mouth recommendation, taken from competitors. Customers won will normally be those who are service literate, that is, demanding and appreciative of the quality benefits, rather than purely price driven. The strategic focus will normally be on these two categories: existing customers and customers gained from rivals.

For companies in new and growing markets, there is the opportunity to expand business through attracting new users. Again the recruitment mechanic relies heavily on endorsement of existing customers and the direct or indirect influence this brings to bear on new users. The skill is in careful management of brand building through product awareness and distribution in support of the innovators. Helping the innovators to 'discover' the product is important. They will not be shown or led. Then ensuring that they pass the message on and the early adopters see the benefits, and buy in imitation. This process is known as 'seeding'. IDV, one of the world's largest drinks companies, has proven proficiency in this area.

Successful brands from IDV like Baileys Irish Cream, Malibu and more recently Archers Peach Schnapps were discreetly seeded into carefully chosen outlets to be effectively 'discovered' by opinion leaders, whose endorsement and recommendation influenced adopters and led progressively to majority acceptance. Advertising only begins at this stage – sooner would deflect the interest of the 'discoverers'. Archers – originally appearing in South Africa – was seeded in the UK in 1988. It only reached a lift-off point for advertising in 1992.

The other category of new users is when the opportunity arises to develop a new segment. This may be in the form of a geographical segment – the extension of Kelloggs Chocos from the French market to the United Kingdom. Alternatively it might be another interpretation of the market segmentation: for example, the launch of 'My First Sony', Walkman, aimed at a new segment of sub-teenage girls. Loyalty building in new segments and among new users takes time and investment.

Loyalty is not a characteristic of the experimental individuals who usually lead consumers into new markets. The essence of experimentation is the thirst for novelty and the preparedness for risk. Neither of these are core dimensions of the loyal customer. The vision is needed to see these fickle triallists as the obligatory springboard to reach the bedrock of secure custom. They are a conduit to the long-run position of the organisation.

The chief executive has the responsibility for ensuring that the organisation understands its options for growth and focuses on a balanced mix of attainable objectives. The primary focus must be to secure absolutely the existing custom, and the additional potential within them. Beyond this the growth will be fuelled by openings in new markets and segments, where patience and strategy will lead to the same basis of loyalty over time.

Positioning

Positioning is the customer's perception of where an organisation stands in relation to its competitors. It is best expressed as a quotation from a customer, asked to describe why one should select one supplier over others.

The ideal positioning adopted by the organisation will reflect the conclusions of two dimensions. The first steer is the understanding of the customers and their needs. What appeal? What set of descriptive advantages would carry them? Secondly, it will take into account the positioning of rivals. The objective is to select a desired positioning which is relevant, motivating to consumers and contrasts with that portrayed by rivals.

EXAMPLES OF OPTIONS FOR POSITIONS

BARGAIN	**Cheapest**
FLEXIBILITY	**Most adaptable**
INNOVATION	**Most creative**
INTEGRITY	**Most trustworthy**
KNOWLEDGE	**Greatest expertise**
MARKET SHARE	**Biggest**
PRESTIGE	**Most exclusive**

QUALITY	**Best made, most reliable**
RELATIONSHIP	**Most committed to customer success**
SERVICE	**Most responsive**
TECHNOLOGY	**First into new technology**
VALUE	**Best price quality performance**
VARIETY	**Widest range**

These examples are simplified. In describing how they perceive a company's position relative to its competitors, customers normally home in on two or just possibly three attributes.

Implementation: the marketing mix and the five Ps

- Product.

- Price.

- Place.

- Promotion.

- People.

An established brand will occupy a position in the minds of its customers. The company may wish to reinforce this or amend it over time. The executional tools for conveying the desired position are the components of the marketing mix. By convention, the marketing mix has four contributors – the so-called Four Ps. To product, price, place (distribution) and promotion, should be added a fifth P. This is 'people', which will almost invariably be part of the differential advantage of a company practising Relationship Marketing. The product/service attributes must stimulate the customer to express the differential advantage in the words of the positioning statement. The communication will need to convey the same values. Price is a signal which justifies the selected position. The distribution channels selected will need to be consistent. Most importantly the behaviours of the people have to personify the positioning. The 'people' include staff directly involved and employed and staff who are behind the scenes or employed by contractors, sub-contractors and support agencies.

The executive role is to thus set the direction and then lead the staff by sharing the vision, utterly convincing everyone to be committed and leading them in the implementation.

Skills for building commitment

The fifth 'P' depends on the commitment of the people concerned. Relationship Marketing does not spring from obedience to external instruction, but internal conviction and motivation. A low level example:

A policy instruction to smile at customers happens at mouth level and comes from the lips. A conviction happens at eye level and comes from the heart.

The skills for building that commitment are essentially five.

- Constructing the vision.

- Communicating interactively.

- Collaborative execution.

- Commitment demonstration.

- Role model reward.

Some thoughts on each in turn.

Constructing the vision

The vision is the inspiring driving force for the organisation. What kind of a team are we? Where are we headed for? How do we work? No one has bettered American writer on business excellence, Tom Peters in his diatribe against the vision – 'We're no worse than anyone else!' In some way, to some group, the organisation has to be the best. It is this belief which engenders pride which drives performance. At the moment of greatest stress under high level demand, with personal abilities stretched, the employee says to herself, 'Why am I doing this?' Alone facing an unscheduled crisis, desperately rectifying the problem three hours after the shift end, the operator says to himself, 'This is way beyond the call of duty!' The realms of duty are well exceeded in these circumstances. Pride in delivering the vision has taken over. I am doing this because we are the best. That is the role of the vision. To sum up the vision: in what respect and for whom, are you the best? Earn the accolade 'world class'.

Communicating interactively

The vision must be shared. Words change their meaning over time. The word 'share' is coming to imply share a concern, or unburden oneself. The concept of sharing a vision is a combination of the older and newer meaning. It means to participate in the exhilaration and excitement, as well as to take on some responsibility for the implementation. The function of communication is to convey the shape of the vision so clearly it can almost be seen, but not so defined that the task is over. Input and contribution are vital. This is so for two reasons. No executive or manager has the ability to know all that the organisation knows. Encouraging input taps what the whole organisation knows collectively. A better answer results. Secondly, the act of contribution – even the invitation to contribute – brings involvement. A personal commitment results.

Information is power. Sharing information is sharing power. Sharing power actually increases it. An organisation where power is delegated has a step function greater leverage than one where power is reserved by the few. Interestingly power is the only commodity that can be increased by division.

As the learning organisation communicates to its customers, listens, modifies its communication and listens again, so does the management function. Executives and managers manage with the benefit of consensus for authority and the quality of contribution for expertise.

Collaborative execution

Interactive communication leads to collaborative execution. The principle is to explain the results required and to create the opportunity to determine method at the level closest to the task. Instructed to roll up the garden hose, my eldest son impressed by creatively spearing three canes in the lawn and running around them with the hose. Result: a neatly rolled hose in less time and no mud on his sleeve. If the operator does not know how to carry out the task better than the manager, then the manager is at fault for selecting the wrong operator. This is involved delegation, not task dumping, for the manager is available as a consultant and coach, but it is not the beacon with all the solutions.

Commitment demonstration

Rather than solving all problems the executive has to personify commitment to the vision. This may be in practical ways, like the managing director heading the product introduction project team personally or signing the document of a major deal after 24 hours of continuous negotiations, red-eyed in a fanfare of publicity. It may be less functional and more theatrical. When the product is launched the chief executive rides as driver's mate for the first delivery. When the plant hits 1,000,000 units, the duty supervisor finds herself whisked by limousine to the boardroom, with the rest of the shift for champagne and strawberries. Everyone knows that the executives are committed. Actions speak louder than words.

Role model rewards

The organisational culture is established by precedent, through the acts of the role models. The management are role models, but throughout the operation there are influential people, junior and senior, young and old, men and women who act as role models. When a new pattern is needed, when changes are taking place, when new initiatives are undertaken, then look for the pioneers of the new practices sought. Find the pioneers, thank them, recognise them and reward them. Catch someone doing it right and celebrate. Celebrate if the pioneer is successful. Show solidarity with the pioneer if the behaviour was right, but the results were not immediately forthcoming.

Commitment

Suddenly, when the commitment is there, the market changes, taxes are raised, a competitor collapses, a scandal erupts . . .

The vision is an unfolding vision. As circumstances change, the direction must be altered. Adjustments are made constantly. Like steering a bicycle, the constant corrections keep the machine in balance and heading in the right direction. The strategy is therefore the collective interpretation of a corporate vision aiming to provide a continuous route in the context of a changing environment.

How does it get there?

Bringing the strategy to fruition and making Relationship Marketing happen through the organisation is the function of the business plan. The thinking behind the business plan is the discernment of resource implications for the execution of the strategic priorities.

The allocating of resources encompasses the human and the financial. With the strategic imperatives in place, the annual plan reviews and sets out the number and skills of the people required, the working capital, investment, borrowings which mean the plan will work in practice.

With a world market for capital, and freer flows of funds across most major markets, finance is not in short supply. The skill is in the management of the return and the perceived risk of the return. The greater the certainty of performance, the lower the risk premium associated with the funding. The message of Relationship Marketing is persuasive to the bankers. The safer returns from loyal customers must be presented with financial acumen that orchestrates and meets expectations.

The human resources plan must cover the potential of the market, the organisational expectations and the aspirations of individuals. Inevitably the conflicting aspects must be resolved. How, for example, with a commitment to Relationship Marketing (which depends on well trained and loyal staff), do you handle a temporary upsurge in business resulting from the collapse of a competitor? How do you address the opposite situation, where a new tax imposition suddenly depresses sales? The one situation implies taking on temporary staff without the standards of permanent staff. The other threatens the security of employment which makes for staff loyalty.

There are no instant answers. There are pointers. The word flexibility is the indicator. The organisation of the end of the century must be able to expand and contract its resources without jeopardising its competencies and commitment.

How can this be done?

Some clues suggest that an organisation has at its core multi-skilled and inspirational leaders, who have on call permanent employees with expertise in a number of roles and flexible contracts of employment. In the first instance work load fluctuations can be met by moving in or redeploying permanent staff from or to other business functions or groups within the firm. Secondly, the flexibility of contracts means that peaks and troughs of work can be addressed by more or less hours of work. Beyond the permanent workforce are two other potential sources of support. There can be contractors and support operations who are briefed, trained and prepared to take on additional tasks. Informally, the organisation can surround itself with individuals who are on call when needed. These may be relatives of staff, former staff, retired people – all of whom are associated with the organisation, but not part of its permanent work force. The web of relationships include people inside the company all the time, some of the time and people in other companies who are equally part of the web.

The discipline of scenario planning is exemplified by Royal Dutch Shell, who use their experts to deliberate on the implications of radically different planning scenarios, for example, how best to respond to a doubling or halving of the world oil price. The same scenario planning is necessary for the human resources aspect of a business.

The business plan is aimed at delivering a smooth flow of income from a regular and established clientele of satisfied customers. The strategic exercises focus the organisation on planning to maintain this smoothness in the context of a world of discontinuous change. On the one hand we have the endeavour. On the other we have the operational reality.

Without Relationship Marketing there will inevitably be more fluctuation in business levels. With it, there is a need for greater flexibility than ever before.

How do you explain this to the staff?

The message to staff is the honest picture:

1 The world is full of surprises which can hit our business.
2 Together we are working to anticipate and smooth the impact of these surprises.
3 We offer openness and our loyalty in return for your flexibility and loyalty.

The Avis slogan of 'We try harder' is an appeal to the car-hiring driver. The same message is the rationale for being part of a company committed to Relationship Marketing. Guaranteed lifetime permanent employment is no more, but we try harder to balance needs of the enterprise and the individuals who form it.

Is the organisation learning as it progresses?

The third management task is to manage the organisational learning, without which the venture withers. The strategic direction and the operational execution are responsibilities which executives accept. As important, is the passionate support for organisational learning. The passion dictates a restless curiosity with every aspect of the operation. How could we run this better? How could we meet these standards at a lower cost? What can we learn from this customer? If this changes, what will be the implication on deliveries? Are there communication channels we have not explored?

- What have I learnt today?

- What have I earned today?

In this double question, is the kernel of the learning organisation. It is everyone's responsibility to search for the new, the unexplored and the yet unknown AND then to look at how this new knowledge can be put into practice to the benefit of staff, customers or shareholders.

The two rules for the chief executive are:

1 Foster curiosity.
2 Promote communication.

Are we getting there?

The fourth task of the chief executive is monitoring the results. The tracking of performance is the absolute strength of the responsive organisation. Countless examples focus on the rate of change. The only way to provide a winning response to changing opportunities is to measure and monitor. Everyone wants to know how they are doing.

Measuring and monitoring

The measurement indicates the performance and subtly it indicates priorities. Measure a sales force on the number of calls made and they rise, monitor mileage and it falls. Too many measures and every member of the sales force decides their own important measure and the effect is dissipated. The conclusion is that the management must measure what is most important. They must inspire individuals and teams to measure themselves on the important criteria.

Easy, visible and short term indicators are reported. The more important measures of the health of the business are neglected. How many 'BUT ALSO' figures can you score?

Not only	But also
Sales revenue levels	Customer satisfaction levels
New accounts won	Account attrition rate
Profit margin	Customer account profitability
Number of customer complaints	Speed of resolution
Head count	Staff turnover rate
New product performance	Percentage of sales from new products

For a different angle on the whole aspect of measurement, Tom Peters has an inspirational section in his handbook, *Thriving on Chaos* (1987). The section is entitled 'Measure What's Important' and includes 20 unconventional measures, most of which will be new to those who have not read that book. My favourite is the 20th: 'What have you changed?'

Back to the beginning again

The fourth executive responsibility leads back to the others. The measurement leads to the need for revisions to strategy, amendments to the plan and finally it charts or challenges the effectiveness of organisational learning.

Bringing it all together is the management task. The explosion of business responsibility at lowest levels of the organisation, driven by the need for customer responsiveness, cost effectiveness and job satisfaction, has also transformed the role of management. Its functions are now visionary, missionary, provisioning, educational and calibrational.

SUMMARY

- The organisation is a directed web of relationships, anticipating and responding to customer needs, and thereby delivering sustainable returns to its shareholders or agreed results to its trustees. Leading the organisation to develop and maintain long-term customer relationships is founded on this web of internal relationships. The task of management is to bring it all together. This embraces constructing the vision which leads to the strategy. The strategy focuses the organisation on attractive markets where it can sustain a differential advantage.

- It also includes the collaboration which develops the business plan or allocation of resources to implement the strategy.

- The third management task is to ensure that the organisation is learning and responding to change.

- Finally, measuring what is important focuses efforts on true priorities and indicates how the organisation is performing.

The measures should reflect the core values of relationship marketing which are all about loyalty and satisfaction delivered by motivated and loyal staff, responsive to changing needs, to keep customers for life.

13

MARKETING: WHERE NEXT?

The future is hard to predict. That it is becoming harder is a theme of this book. For this reason, much stress has been laid upon the need for understanding customers and their changing needs so well that it is possible to anticipate them. The accent is on close relationships and emotional empathy with customers on one side, and responsiveness and speed of execution on the other. In this way it is possible to know quickly what is wanted and provide it in an accelerated manner. The backdrop is a willingness to experiment and a restlessness for novelty. Even when customers cannot be anticipated, they can be stimulated to react to developments and extensions and innovations. Some of these will lead the market in new directions.

Relationship Marketing is vivacious marketing

Marketing which empathises with customers, where supplier and customer get close to each other, where there is dialogue and quick response and where novelty and interest are welcomed is best described as vivacious. It is lively. It is stimulating. It is fast moving. Above all it is fun.

Where next?

Vivacious Relationship Marketing is the organisation's best response to the changes which are taking place. It best serves the expectations of all the stakeholders of the organisation – shareholders, employees, customers, suppliers and distributors and dependents of all of these. Change is endemic. Discontinuous change, radical change, accelerating change. The greatest function the organisation can perform in this environment, is to represent a picture of certainty.

Reliability in the face of uncertainty

When the world is an uncertain place, there is delight in finding an element of near certainty. Someone who can be relied upon. Someone who is up-to-date and can translate what that now means. A guide and interpreter to trends and their benefits or risks. The reliable organisation is not fixed and unchanging. In fact part of its reliability is that it is never left behind.

Businesses are ships in convoy, crossing the ocean

To continue a previous allusion, it is like a mother ship of a convoy across an ocean. Through experience and contact with the whole convoy, it has a clearer view of the direction to sail, the speed to make progress and the risks to be tackled *en route*. To the ships of the convoy, it represents safety in adversity and they aim to steam close to that mother ship, staying with it for the duration.

What can we predict?

Despite the difficulties, there are some trends which can be discerned. I will consider changes taking place in sales and marketing.

A prediction about marketing

The role of marketing is changing. For 30 years or more it has been seen as a business function which was handled by a specialist department. Quality formerly rested within a department in many concerns. It progressed to become a management issue on the agenda of every departmental manager. Now quality has come out of its department beyond the management layer and is seen as the responsibility of every person in the organisation. From the quality manual and standards procedure, we are moving to the daily interpretation and development of quality as an evolving item. It is not fixed for ever, it is a living response to external change or stimuli and internal initiative.

Everyone is a marketer

Like quality, Marketing is coming out of its department. Of course there are still specialists, but it is moving to become the responsibility of everyone in the organisation. Market research has its specialist techniques, but much of the customer information needed is held in the minds of people who have customer contact, or observe the direction of the customers' expectations.

Teams working together, not functions in sequence

Product development needs careful assessment by specialists. However, the organisation additionally needs the knowledge, ingenuity and commitment of a multi-functional group to enhance the existing range and develop new products. Research published by the Boston Consulting Group in 1993 showed the survey results of 600 companies in Europe, Japan and the United States of America. Clearly it demonstrated that speed to market of new products was the best predictor for profitable performance. Products brought to market faster turned out to be better than those with a longer gestation period. How could this be? The answer is that to bring out a new product quickly you must have collaboration with simultaneous development by research, design, marketing, production, operations, finance and sales. Sequential development by each of the functions with a stake in the project results in slower development, more revisions and a poorer product at the end of the day. Conversely, if all departments are represented in a single development team, the result is faster *and* better.

No monopoly of communications with customers

Communications is another marketing department responsibility which is moving to the whole organisation. The increasing service element with every product, brings more people into contact with customers. If there is a phone help line, then that operator is as much part of the marketing communications as the advertising campaign. Every part of the organisation is communicating directly or indirectly with customers. The strategy must be understood and executed consistently by all communicators. Marketing are custodians of the message, but have no monopoly of communications.

The sales function is changing too

The sales process, like the marketing department, is now involving the rest of the organisation. The historic pattern of the representative in a lone role winning the order from a retailer or industrial company is no longer appropriate for most businesses. The selling operation is now a co-ordination task.

The three stage co-ordination: Before, during and after

Prior to the sale, the client or customer, there is an analytical requirement. What is needed? What is the problem? What solutions are possible? Which will meet the long-term needs most cost effectively? The representative is a contact point, calling in technical support from across the company, or even outside it. The sale itself has legal, logistical and commercial considerations. All these could be best handled by a specific expert. Finally, after delivery there may be an installation to be arranged with checks and tests. The customer may have staff to be trained. Many forms of after sales service exist. For example, consultancy may maintain lowest cost in use for the buyer.

Conducting an orchestra of technical support

The sales representative is like the conductor of an orchestra. The role is the complex careful assessment of the most appropriate service provider within the organisation for a specific part of the sales process. The expert then needs briefing and introducing to the client. All the advice and guidance must be compatible. At the same time the style and approach of all must be in sympathy with the identity of the company and the needs of the buying organisation.

What this means for the organisation

There are three interesting conclusions of these two examples of change. The first is that across the organisation more people are becoming multi-functional in their outlook. The functional barriers are breaking down. An integrated view is the only possible one. Secondly, team working is the only way forward. No single person has the knowledge of the customer, the product, the process and the available options. More and more operations are turning to teams to run them. These may be formally established or informal groupings. They may even be self managing. Finally, following the last point, seniority is secondary to role. In other words, the sales representative may be the most junior individual in the team supporting the winning of a contract. Yet it is possible that senior experts, even top executives may be on call to deliver the service determined necessary by the representative. Who works for whom?

Organisational changes

- Functional divisions are disappearing.

- Individuals are acting as team members.

- Seniority is secondary to role.

These changes are taking place in the organisations you buy from and sell to. The complexity of two organisations (both becoming structured in these new ways) trading and working together is challenging. The previous solutions of mass marketing, mass communication, standardisation for cost reduction and so on are thoroughly outmoded.

Relationship Marketing is the future

The conclusion must be that the best future for an organisation is to operate the laid-out guidelines of Relationship Marketing.

The right staff are loyal staff

Begin with the organisational framework which includes the right staff. The right staff are selected for their loyalty quotient. All things being equal, with their characteristics they are more likely to remain with you and stay motivated in the culture of the organisation you run.

Loyal customers too

Study the market, seek out the segments which have the highest pre-disposition to loyalty. Increase the emphasis on these customer types. Recruit customers deliberately for their loyalty potential. Invest in them and earn their long-term business.

Learn, learn, learn

Earning long-term business means customers must have confidence in you as a supplier today and in the future. This means that you must learn their true and underlying needs by being close to them. Visit, observe and listen – then react to meet those needs. It is your skills at anticipation of the market, which adds real value and secures their lifetime relationship with you.

Price for the slow buck

There is a huge value to the organisation from the greater profitability that long term relationships bring. There are huge savings to be made when you do not keep churning customers. Your long-term customers know this. Part of the unspoken contract is that you will share some of the profit benefits with your loyal customers. This sharing is often expressed as constant extensions of value.

Dialogue not monologue

Continuing communication assists in building the strength depth and durability of the relationship. It is interactive communications with listening as well as speaking. It is frequent: uses all the varied means of keeping in touch held together by a consistent style. It is as personal as the market conditions permit. It hits the right note with the recipient. The communications and organisational behaviour stimulates word-of-mouth marketing. Customers extend your sales force by marketing you to like minded potential customers.

Service makes the difference

The people in the organisation are the differentiators in a world of parity products and 'overnight' replication of product attributes. The service standard is harder to emulate. Through training, development, coaching and role models, you can distance yourself from rivals. The service makes the relationship which keeps customers for life.

Bringing it all together

The chief executive officer brings together the web of relationships which form an organisation. The unification needs a uniting vision, a cause to strive for. This leads to a strategy focusing on the building of relationships. Planning and implementation are collaborative activities, maximising corporate knowledge and commitment. To know whether it has all been brought together, measurement is essential. Measure the important things – most businesses measure the easily calibrated ratios, rather than the grades which make the difference.

A man who exemplifies this

There is a man who has been running a business employing these principles, intuitively. I have observed him as a customer for more than twenty years. I cannot imagine anything causing me to move my business. He is my dentist. He never advertised – in those days, it was not permissable to do so. When I moved to Oxford, I was recommended to his practice by the mother of a friend who lived locally. Through word-of-mouth marketing I became a patient. His excellent skills at dentistry caused his practice to expand, and he was always careful to select patients who cared for their teeth enough to look after them and attend regular check ups. Not for him the ephemeral customers with emergency toothache problems stemming from their own neglect.

He has staff who exude the same confidence as he himself provides. They are warm and welcoming. I remember a sullen hygienist who had left by the time of my next appointment. He always seems up-to-date. A new piece of equipment here, a new approach there. I have a conviction that his dentistry reflects the best practice of the profession. He would never be left behind.

He has a large practice, yet he knows me as an individual. He always he has a pertinent welcoming greeting, perhaps related to my business, my family or my interests. Once he was amused by my appearance on his television screen a few weeks beforehand. Dialogue in the dental chair is not easy. Somehow it happens. Surprisingly, I look forward to my visits. Wherever I have lived, London, Lancashire, Sydney, Seattle, he has remained my dentist.

In a crisis he is there. To attend to my second son's broken front tooth, he kept his surgery open into the evening. Before he touched the tooth, he took time to relax my son with explanation and reassurance.

Mr Farrant personifies Relationship Marketing for me.

INDEX

Further titles of interest

FINANCIAL TIMES

PITMAN PUBLISHING

ISBN	TITLE	AUTHOR
0 273 60561 5	Achieving Successful Product Change	Innes
0 273 03970 9	Advertising on Trial	Ring
0 273 60232 2	Analysing Your Competitor's Financial Strengths	Howell
0 273 60466 X	Be Your Own Management Consultant	Pinder
0 273 60168 7	Benchmarking for Competitive Advantage	Bendell
0 273 60529 1	Business Forecasting using Financial Models	Hogg
0 273 60456 2	Business Re-engineering in Financial Services	Drew
0 273 60069 9	Company Penalties	Howarth
0 273 60558 5	Complete Quality Manual	McGoldrick
0 273 03859 1	Control Your Overheads	Booth
0 273 60022 2	Creating Product Value	De Meyer
0 273 60300 0	Creating World Class Suppliers	Hines
0 273 60383 3	Delayering Organisations	Keuning
0 273 60171 7	Does Your Company Need Multimedia?	Chatterton
0 273 60003 6	Financial Engineering	Galitz
0 273 60065 6	Financial Management for Service Companies	Ward
0 273 60205 5	Financial Times Guide to Using the Financial Pages	Vaitilingam
0 273 60006 0	Financial Times on Management	Lorenz
0 273 03955 5	Green Business Opportunities	Koechlin
0 273 60385 X	Implementing the Learning Organisation	Thurbin
0 273 03848 6	Implementing Total Quality Management	Munro-Faure
0 273 60025 7	Innovative Management	Phillips
0 273 60327 2	Investor's Guide to Emerging Markets	Mobius
0 273 60622 0	Investor's Guide to Measuring Share Performance	Macfie
0 273 60528 3	Investor's Guide to Selecting Shares that Perform	Koch
0 273 60704 9	Investor's Guide to Traded Options	Ford
0 273 03751 X	Investor's Guide to Warrants	McHattie
0 273 03957 1	Key Management Ratios	Walsh
0 273 60384 1	Key Management Tools	Lambert
0 273 60259 4	Making Change Happen	Wilson
0 273 60424 4	Making Re-engineering Happen	Obeng
0 273 60533 X	Managing Talent	Sadler
0 273 60153 9	Perfectly Legal Competitor Intelligence	Bernhardt
0 273 60167 9	Profit from Strategic Marketing	Wolfe
0 273 60170 9	Proposals, Pitches and Beauty Parades	de Forte
0 273 60616 6	Quality Tool Kit	Mirams
0 273 60336 1	Realising Investment Value	Bygrave
0 273 60713 8	Rethinking the Company	Clarke
0 273 60328 0	Spider Principle	Linton
0 273 03873 7	Strategic Customer Alliances	Burnett
0 273 03949 0	Strategy Quest	Hill
0 273 60624 7	Top Intrapreneurs	Lombriser
0 273 03447 2	Total Customer Satisfaction	Horovitz
0 273 60201 2	Wake Up and Shake Up Your Company	Koch
0 273 60387 6	What Do High Performance Managers Really Do?	Hodgson

For further details or a full list of titles contact:

The Professional Marketing Department, Pitman Publishing, 128 Long Acre, London WC2E 9AN, UK

Tel +44 (0)71 379 7383 or fax +44 (0)71 240 5771